Introduction to
Glass Fusing

by Petra Kaiser

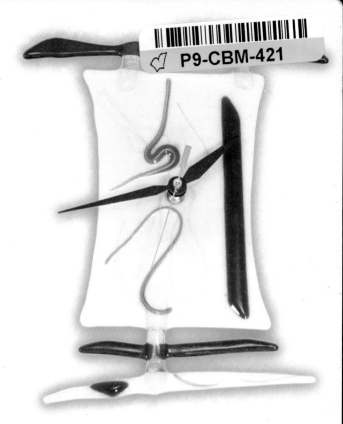

An illustrated tutorial on the techniques of art glass fusing. Filled with easy to follow step-by-step photos, useful 'HotTip' sidebars and complete project instructions.

Wardell
PUBLICATIONS INC

Photo left: Necklace pendants featuring Dichroic coated glass with a captivating intensity that can turn an ordinary project into an absolute work of art all by itself.

Cataloging in Publication Data

Kaiser, Petra
Introduction to Glass Fusing : project-by-project guided lessons
Author: Petra Kaiser; glass craft;
Includes index.

ISBN 0-919985-38-6

1. Glass fusing. I. Title.

TT298.K33 2003 748.2'028 C2003-903284-1

Printed and bound in Thailand by Phongwarin Printing Ltd.
Published simultaneously in Canada and USA
Distributed worldwide, inquire for dealer list
P. O. Box 480069 Fort Lauderdale, FL 33348-0069 USA
E-mail: info@wardellpublications.com • Website: www.wardellpublications.com

Introduction to

Glass Fusing

Author
Petra Kaiser

Fabrication Assistance
Wolfgang Kaiser

Photography
Wolfgang Kaiser and Randy Wardell

Digital Photo Retouching
Randy Wardell and Jillian Sandler

Text Editor
Randy Wardell

Book Layout & Typography
Randy Wardell and Carole Wardell

Publisher
Randy Wardell

Acknowledgements

First I want to thank those individuals who were directly involved in putting this book together, Randy and Carole Wardell and of course my husband Wolfgang. The list of people who influenced and encouraged me is too long to mention but it includes all my teachers, students, friends and moral supporters. I thank you all!

I also want to thank Ron Bearer Sr., for giving us a head start with our product, by inviting us to our first distributor open house. That opportunity was our introduction to the many great people in the art glass industry and it helped us to become part of a worldwide community united by the passion for art glass.

Published by

Wardell
PUBLICATIONS INC

Send your comments and suggestions or sign-up to receive our "New Editions" digital newsletter.
Contact us by E-mail: info@wardellpublications.com or visit our Website at: www.wardellpublications.com

A Message from the Author

I have had many experiences in my life and I'd have to say that glass fusing has definitely been a highlight for me (of course meeting and marrying my husband Wolfgang is up there as well). I want to thank the City of Cape Coral, Florida for offering a fusing course in their recreation center and also my first teacher Jaunita Deck, for introducing me to the art of fusing.

The two themes that have consistently run through my career life are being creative and working with people. The wonderful medium of 'art glass' has fulfilled both of these aspects magnificently. My formal education is in teaching and I spent many years instructing practical secretarial and office management skills to post high-school students. That experience has helped me to structure my glass fusing workshops and this instruction book.

I enjoy traveling and glass fusing provides the opportunity to both give and attend educational workshops. I find it is one of the best ways to meet people that share my interest in creativity and art. My circle of new friends most often comes from these experiences and the inspirations we get from working together is a big plus. I have come to realize that working with glass has not only changed my life, but the lives of many others. Perhaps the life altering quality is due to the limitless diversity and opportunities that we have in kiln fired glass.

From jewelry to tableware, from sculptures to wall art, from shower doors to sinks, and beyond into your mind's eye. Warm glass art is here for us to enjoy and all it takes is a little knowledge, a kiln and some imagination.

Petra Kaiser

Author Contact Information:

Kaiser Glass Design Studio
3732 SE 21st Place, Cape Coral, Florida 33904 USA
Ph: 239.540.1137
E-Mail: kaiserlee@earthlink.net
Website: www.kaiser-lee-glass-art.com

TABLE OF CONTENTS

CHAPTER ONE

Introduction

Glass Fusing

In the ancient world of 1500 BC to 500 BC glass was the exclusive domain of the monarchy and privileged citizens of the day and was an important aspect for the control of power and wealth. Glassmakers were held in very high regard and the process itself was a closely guarded secret. Now thousands of years later, we have refined the technique of glass fusing and the opportunity to create glass objects is now within reach of anyone with the desire to learn. The materials, tools and techniques are readily available and with some basic instruction we can all take on the dominion of the privileged glassmakers, even in our own kitchens and workshops.

The inspiration for this fused and slump formed mask set was a stained glass pattern published in Spectrum's Score Magazine.

Instant Gratification!

Glass is a magnificent material for the artist. It's difficult to create something in glass that is unattractive. Those who are not familiar with the technique of fusing will gaze in wonderment and disbelief when you show them your first fused "object d'art" and tell them you made it yourself.

We are grateful to the modern pioneers who have lead the way to develop and refine the technique in partnership with the industry to provide the right material and equipment. Glass fusing, or warm glass as it is also known, is readily accessible to everyone from commission artists to hobby level crafters.

Glass

People seem to be fascinated by glass, especially colored glass. I think it has to do with the combination of the rainbow reflection and refraction of the light, the glossy shine and its' versatility. When I first heard the term 'art glass fusing' I had no real idea what that meant, but the words 'art glass' definitely got my attention.

In modern society, glass is literally everywhere. It's mind blowing to think of all the everyday items that are made out of glass. Imagine a home without glass. We use glass for windows, cabinet doors, shelves, tabletops, bottles, drinking glasses, vases, cookware, light bulbs, eyeglasses, far too many applications to mention. The industrial and technical use of glass is almost beyond imagination; glass is crucial in medical & scientific laboratories, space exploration, and machinery of every kind. The world as we know it would collapse - quite literally, if we did not have glass.

This product, that is so indispensable, is created from surprisingly basic and commonplace components. The main ingredients are: sand, limestone and sodium carbonate. Color is added using various metal oxides and other mineral components.

Throughout history glass has not always been accessible for artists to choose it as a working medium. Today artists are no longer confined by tradition and regulations of the material and have a wide range of glass working techniques available for them to realize their artistic concepts.

A short list would include; glass casting, core forming, lamp worked glass, glass blowing, stained glass, glass fusing, glass etching, glass mosaics, staining and painting on glass, to name only a few.

CHAPTER TWO

Warm Glass Processes

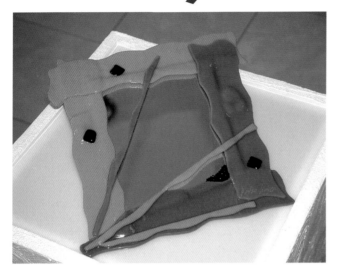

This decorator mirror was created by tack fusing a selection of narrow border pieces. We created the indent space from the back by slumping the frame over a piece of fiber paper. The mirror glass was added after fusing using E6000™ adhesive.

This book will concentrate on glass fusing techniques, also known as (a.k.a.) warm glass or kiln formed glass. Various processes and effects are possible by carefully controlling the temperature and time during firing of the kiln. The terminology and definitions for each of these are described in the following chart.

Temperatures listed are general guidelines for illustration purposes only. The temperatures given are typical for fusible art glasses. Other kinds of glass may require different temperatures.

Actual firing temperatures and time schedules will be specified for each project in the book. Combing, pate de verre and glass casting are techniques we will discuss in future books.

Process	Fahrenheit / Celsius	Definition
Draping	1200°F to 1250°F 650°C to 675°C	Shaping glass by heating it until it bends over a mold, under its own weight.
Fire polishing	1300°F to 1400°F 705°C to 760°C	Heating glass to the point where the edges round off and are left with a shiny appearance.
Slumping	1300°F to 1450°F 705°C to 790°C	Shaping glass by heating it until it stretches and drops (slumps) into a mold.
Tack fusing	1350°F to 1450°F 730°C to 790°C	Heating the glass to the point where the individual components begin to stick together, with each piece retaining its individual shape and character.
Full fusing	1450°F to 1550°F 790°C to 845°C	Merge two or more layers of glass by heating and temperature soaking until the glass is fully combined.
Frit casting	1480°F to 1600°F 805°C to 870°C	Small crushed pieces of glass (called 'frit') are placed inside a dam mold to control the shape and fired to full-fuse.
Pate de Verré	1500°F to 1600°F 815°C to 870°C	Finely ground glass is emulsified, placed into a special mold and kiln-fired to form a solid glass sculptural shape.
Combing	1650°F to 1750°F 900°C to 955°C	Glass is softened to almost-molten state and is manipulated by "raking" a metal tool across the surface to "comb" the colors into various patterns.
Glass Casting	1700°F to 1800°F 925°C to 980°C	Glass is melted in a crucible to a liquid state then it is poured into a specially prepared mold.

CHAPTER THREE

About This Book

If you're like me, you will want to get to work on your first project right away. That is why I will keep the theory part as short as possible. Each chapter will feature a variety of techniques on certain subjects. As you work through the projects step-by-step you'll acquire the basic knowledge for glass fusing. In this way your technical skills will advance with each project you are making.

One of my hobbies is cooking. I enjoy reading and trying out new recipes from a variety of cookbooks. When I first started to cook I had no choice but to follow the instructions exactly if I wanted the dish to be successful. Now, with experience (and a few mishaps) I only need to quickly read through the ingredients list and browse the directions to discern how I'm going to prepare the dish.

Chapters 4 through 6 of this book provide information on the specialty materials, tools and equipment that are essential for this craft. You will also find technical instructions for glass cutting, shaping and other pre-fusing preparation techniques. These sections are particularly important if you have not worked with glass before. Chapter 8 presents 15 complete projects with a tools & materials list plus detailed and easy to follow 'step-by-step' project instructions.

So the idea behind this book is to create a basic glass fusing 'cookbook'. I recommend that you at least read through each project even if you don't want to 'cook' the item. Each project focuses on specific subject matters to give you practical tips, technical advice and rules to follow. Later, with the help of the index, you can use the book as a reference guide to refresh your memory.

CHAPTER FOUR

Tools Equipment & Supplies

Let's start with the minimum requirements for your glass fusing shop area. The following list is an overview of the items found in most glass fusing workshops. You don't need everything on this list to get started and some of the items on the list are available in numerous model types and styles. It's always a good idea to ask your friendly local retail supplier for their recommendation before making your purchase.

Design Concept Utensils

• Paper, Ruler, Pencil, Scissors - and whatever else you might need to record your great ideas

Glass Storage

• Upright wooden bins, custom glass racks or a Morton Glass Caddy

• Containers - for small glass pieces (i.e. plastic parts bins); keep glass sorted into COE & color groups

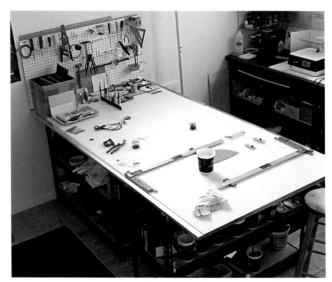

This is a photo of the workbench in our glass preparation area. Notice the tool rack at the end that keeps most of our hand tools within easy reach. We've also created an extensive built-in storage under the bench. With a little ingenuity you can have a complete fusing workshop within a very compact space.

1. Glass Caddy with Glass
2. Plastic 'Cafeteria-Style' Tray
3. Rubbing Alcohol
4. White Bond Glue
5. Grozing Pliers
6. Breaker/Grozer Pliers
7. Solid Cutting Surface
8. Permanent Markers
9. Paper, Ruler, Pencil, Scissors
10. Container for Small Glass Pcs
11. Kiln Vent & Small Shelf
12. Tweezers, Bent-nose
13. Running Pliers
14. Glass Cutter, Professional
15. Glass Cutter Storage Jar
16. Morton Cutting Surface

Glass Cutting

- Worktable - for glass cutting and preparation
- Glass Cutting Surface - e.g. Morton surface that provides pockets to catch small glass chips
- Solid Cutting Surface - for smaller pieces, e.g. soft tile board (the type used for drop ceilings)
- Permanent Markers - black, silver &/or white to draw on glass
- Glass Cutter - professional model with carbide wheel, available in several handle styles, see page 18
- Glass Cutter Storage Container - a coffee mug or small glass jar with a cotton rag on the inside bottom, soaked with glass cutter oil
- Glass Cutter Oil - Novacan Cutter Oil, Enviro Gold Cutting Fluid, GlassPro Cutting Fluid, etc.
- Glass Pliers - running pliers, breaker/grozer pliers
- Morton Safety Break System - helps to make glass breaking more reliable and consistent

Project Assembly

- Adhesives (used for pre-fire assembly) - Hotline Fusers Glue, Klyr Fire Glue, &/or White bond glue
- Tweezers, with bent nose - used for placing small décor glass pieces on your work

Preparing and Cleaning

- Soft Cloth - you will need a supply of fabric cloths to use for cleaning at various stages in the fusing process. I like to use cotton dishcloths but many fusers use old towels, T-shirts or similar types of cotton material, cut into assorted sizes.
- Plastic Dish Wash Basin - approximately 10" x 14" x 5" deep (25 x 36 x 13 cm deep) this will be used to soak and wash your glass components prior to firing
- Plastic Trash Bucket - approximately 8" x 14" x 12" deep (20 x 36 x 30 cm deep) this will be used to soak and wash your glass projects after firing, see HotTip 'Dunk Bucket' on page 31
- Cleaners - Isopropyl Alcohol (rubbing alcohol), Dish washing detergent, Goof Off™ (used to remove sticky residue)

A selection of cleaning supplies that we use constantly are; dish wash detergent, Isopropyl alcohol & Goof-Off™ to remove stains & sticker residue.

White bond glue for pre-fusing assembly and E6000™ to mount finished

CHAPTER FOUR - Tools & Supplies

Fusing, Slumping, Draping, Fire Polishing

- Kiln; various models available - see Kilns and Controllers on pages 11-14
- Kiln Controller; to regulate temperature - see Kiln Controllers on page 11
- Kiln Shelf - made from Mullite clay, see page 15
- Small Piece of Fiberboard - to vent the kiln
- Kitchen Timer - for kiln sitting
- Kiln Wash (a.k.a. Shelf Primer - kiln preparation is an important step in glass fusing and the best shelf primer product to use is a matter of considerable discussion among fusers. Some commonly available primers are: Primo Primer, Hotline Shelf Primer, Hi-Fire Shelf Primer, Bullseye Shelf Primer, and Unique Glass Separator to name only a few

Safety Supplies

- Safety Eyeglasses or Goggles
- Hi Temperature Kiln Gloves
- Respiratory Mask

Power Tools and Accessories

- Glass Grinder - table top machine designed to grind and shape glass
- Grinding Head, Diamond - standard grit in standard size for your machine
- Drilling Head, Diamond - 1/8" & 1/4" (3 & 6 mm)
- High-speed Hand Drill - minimum 20,000 rpm
- Diamond Coated Hollow Core Drill Bits, sizes: - 5/64" (2 mm), 1/4" (6 mm) & 5/16" (8 mm)
- Shallow Plastic 'cafeteria-style' Tray - approximately 10" x 14" x 3/4" deep (25 x 36 x 2 cm deep) used when drilling holes in glass (see page 32)

Clockwise from bottom left; kiln shelf supports both short and tall, insulation kiln brick, and small Mullite kiln shelf.

Clockwise from top; 2 types of kiln wash, small strainer, nylon stocking filled with kiln wash, hake brush with mixing bowl.

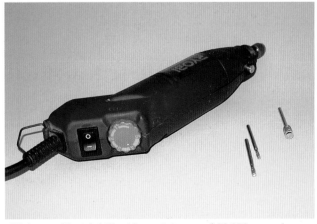

High-speed hand drill with a minimum of 20,000 rpm, shown with 3 sizes of hollow core diamond drill bits.

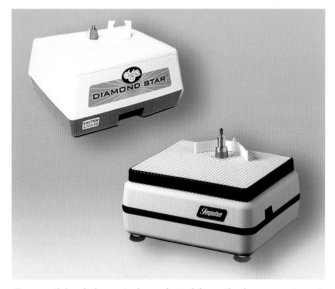

Two models of glass grinders selected from the large assortment of hobby-duty grinders now available.

Introduction to Glass Fusing

Kilns, Controllers & Accessories

The purchase of a glass kiln is the largest single investment you will have to make in glass fusing. Therefore it is important to make an informed choice. There are dozens of different kilns available and new ones are introduced regularly. I could not possibly describe all the options that are offered, that would be a book all by itself. Instead I will list some of the things that you'll need to consider to help you ask the right questions when you are talking to the kiln sales representative. In addition you will find a catalog of assorted entry-level kilns with descriptions and photographs, provided to me by the respective manufacturers (see pages 12-14).

Size Matters

The first question that you'll need to answer is what size and kinds of items do you intend to create? This will be a key factor to determine the size and type of kiln. For example if you are primarily interested in making jewelry items or perhaps small trays or tiles then a kiln with an interior dimension of 6" up to 12" would suffice. However if you think you will want to make larger plates, bowls, masks, etc. then a medium sized kiln from 14" to 20" would be a better purchase. Ultimately you may want to move up to a professional style kiln from 24" diameter, or an oval kiln measuring 20" x 30" or perhaps even a rectangle kiln in the 24" x 36" range or even larger. My advice would be that you can never go wrong having one of the smaller size kilns. Then purchase a larger one later on when you have practiced your skills and want to move on to more advanced projects. The smaller kilns are always better for jewelry making and they're ideal for slumping and draping smaller projects. You will also find the smaller kilns come in handy to make fused components that will be combined later into one project using a larger kiln.

Electrical Considerations

Kilns have a variety of electrical requirements. You will need to take into account the type of electrical feed that you have in the workroom where you intend to install the kiln. It is very important that the voltage, amperage and wiring are matched to the requirement of the kiln and that it complies with the electrical code in your area. Be sure to consult a professional electrician. In the interest of safety the kiln must to be set away from all flammable surfaces and must be properly wired.

Shape and Lid Position

Kilns are available in 3 basic shapes, round (actually 6, 7 or 8 sided), square, and rectangle. Of course there are modifications on these shapes (i. e. ovals) and each shape is available in a range of depths. Most kilns are top loading where the lid is hinged mounted and positioned on the topside, some models have removable lids (no hinge) and still others are hinged at the bottom (clamshell). Front loading kilns have a hinged side door for access to the firing chamber. Each model has its advantages so be sure to ask the sales associate at your local store for more details.

Heating Elements

Most electric glass fusing kilns have heating elements positioned in the walls and in the topside (usually the lid) as well. However some models have elements in the sidewalls only and others have them in topside only. Again there are advantages to all these styles so ask your fusing supply center for assistance.

Kiln Controllers

Obviously you will need a way to turn the kiln on and off but of course it's not always that simple. Small kilns usually have a dial type controller switch with

several power level positions and a pyrometer (hi-temp thermometer) to enable the operator to determine the various firing stages. Medium and larger kilns normally have multiple switches with a pyrometer or may come equipped with a digital controller. They can be programmed to automatically run the temperature up at a specified rate, hold a specific temperature for a set period of time and then allow the kiln to cool at the required rate for optimum annealing (relieving internal stress) of the glass.

CHAPTER FIVE - Kilns, Controllers & Accessories

Which kiln is the right one for you?

The selection and purchase of your kiln is vital. It is the most important tool in the glass fusing process and many factors must be taken into consideration prior to making your decision. Consult with other fusers and ask their opinion on various kiln types. Talk to the sales representative and do some research at the websites of the various kiln manufacturers to get as much information as you can. Your kiln is an important and major investment that necessitates some determined research. The following section provides a list of the entry-level kilns that are currently available. The information is a basic description provided by the manufacturers and we are not recommending any particular kiln over another. It really does come down to a personal choice. We have provided the website address for each manufacturer so you can check for up-to-the-minute information before you make your final decision.

Olympic - 126GF

This kiln features separate functioning elements in the lid and sidewalls for maximum heating power and uses a 120volt - 20amp circuit (a special outlet). The 126GF is available in either top loading or clamshell loading configuration. The optional RTC 1000

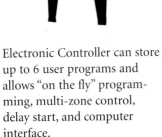

Electronic Controller can store up to 6 user programs and allows "on the fly" programming, multi-zone control, delay start, and computer interface.

• Firing Chamber Dimensions: 11.25" diameter x 6" deep (28.6 cm diameter x 16.5 cm deep)

http://www. kilns-kilns.com/

Evenheat - Hot Shot

The Hot Shot combines the space and performance of a large kiln with the convenience of standard 120volt - 15amp operation. The Hot Shot is equipped with Evenheat's Set-Pro, 3 button controller that allows up to 8 changes in temperature, speed and hold times per firing plus "on the fly" features to give you complete control.

• Firing Chamber Dimensions: 14.5" diameter x 6.5" deep (37 cm diameter x 16.5 cm deep)

Evenheat - Hot Box

This handy little kiln is useful for small fusing projects or small design elements. It comes with a manually controlled infinite switch and pyrometer and operates on a standard 120volt - 15amp outlet. The Hot Box is available with an optional viewing window built into the lid to give a full view of your glass during the firing process.

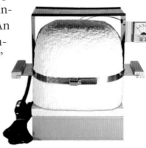

• Firing Chamber Dimensions: 6" square x 4.5" deep (15.2 cm square x 11.4 cm deep)

Evenheat - Rapid Fire 6

The small, lightweight Rapid Fire 6 is great for jewelry and small items. Stock equipped with a manually controlled in-line switch and pyrometer. An optional Infinite Switch Controller allows you to "dial in" a heat setting for more precision. Plug the kiln into the controller and the controller into a standard 120volt - 15amp circuit and it's ready.

• Firing Chamber Dimensions: 6" square x 6" deep (15.2 cm square x 15.2 cm deep)

http://www. evenheat-kiln.com/

AIM - 1406LE Fusing Kiln.

This kiln has heating elements in the side and lid, each with a separate infinite-switch control. It operates on a standard 120 volt 15 amps electrical circuit to achieve 1600°F (871°C). AIM offers 3 optional controllers to give you precise and consistent temperature regulation of your kiln for predictable and repeatable results. The Fuji PXV-3 Digital set-point controller with a programmable, four segment program, the 3-Key controller by Bartlett Instruments is an easy to use, multi-program controller with memory for 4 programs, and the V6-CF controller by Bartlett Instruments, a 10 numbered key pad with both pre-programmed schedules and programmable user defined firing profiles.

• Firing Chamber Dimensions: 14" diameter x 6.5" deep (28.6 cm diameter x 15.2 cm deep)

AIM -84J Mini Kiln

This portable kiln is useful for many smaller projects and jewelry components. The elements are in the sidewalls and operate on a standard 120volt - 15amp outlet. An infinite control switch and pyrometer are standard (an optional digital controller is available). This kiln can be modified for bead makers' by adding the optional lower ring with a 2" x 6" (5 x 15 cm) door, allowing it to be used for bead rod pre-heating.

• Firing Chamber Dimensions: 8" square x 4.5" deep (20.3 cm square x 15.2 cm deep)

http://www. aimkilns.com/

Paragon - Fusion-7

The Fusion-7 hot glass kiln operates on a standard 120volt - 15amp circuit and includes a built-in digital Sentry Xpress controller that features a simple 3-key operation with an 8-segment program sophisticated enough for professional use. This 7-sided model has heating elements in top, a peephole in the side, a lock-in lid support and a steel stand.

• Firing Chamber Dimensions: 14.5" diameter x 6.5" deep (37 cm diameter x 16.5 cm deep)

Paragon - QuikFire 6

The QuikFire 6 has a ceramic fiber upper shell with an embedded heating element. The upper section rests on a ceramic fiber base with a formed steel stand. It fires on standard 120volt - 15amp outlet and uses only 1560 watts, less power than many hair driers. An optional Infinite Control Switch allows you to slow the QuikFire for more precision.

• Firing Chamber Dimensions: 6" square x 6" deep (15.2 cm square x 15.2 cm deep)

Paragon - Caldera

This side element kiln has a removable top lid and base and uses a standard 120volt - 15amp outlet. The Sentry Xpress controller is included to control both heating and cooling with simple 3-key operation. This kiln offers a bonus for glass bead-makers'; an optional collar can be added to the base unit to provide a 7.5" x 2" (19 x 5 cm) door to permit bead rod pre-heating.

• Firing Chamber Dimensions: 8" square x 6" deep (20.3 cm square x 15.2 cm deep)

http://www. paragonweb.com/

Jen Ken - Fusing & Bead Annealer

This 6-sided kiln has heating elements in the sidewalls only and operates on a standard 120volt - 15amp outlet. A infinite control switch and pyrometer are standard. A digital controller is available as an option. This kiln is also available with an extra lower ring that has a built-in 2" x 6" (5 x 15 cm) lower side door that enhances its' role as a glass bead annealer.

• Firing Chamber Dimensions: 11" diameter x 4.5" deep (28 cm diameter x 11.5 cm deep)

Jen Ken - B3K-15/6

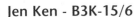

This 7-sided kiln has heating elements in the lid and sidewalls that operate on a 120volt - 20amp circuit (a special outlet). The 3-button Digital controller is standard equipment and has 4 user programs with 8 segments each to automatically control the ramp rate, soak temperature, hold times, and cooling cycle, allowing the operator to choose the value for each component.

• Firing Chamber Dimensions: 15" diameter x 6" deep (38 cm diameter x 15 cm deep)

Jen Ken - AF3P Topfire-11/6

This is the little brother to the Jen Ken-15/6 kiln (shown above). It is built the same and has a similar 3-button Digital controller. The difference is the firing chamber is 4" (10.2 cm) smaller in diameter and it has the heating element in the lid only. In addition it can operate on a standard 120volt - 15amp outlet.

• Firing Chamber Dimensions: 11" diameter x 6" deep (28 cm diameter x 15 cm deep)

Note: Both kilns are available with either the B3K or the AF3P Digital Controller installed.

http://www.jenkenkilns.com/

System 96 - HotStart by Skutt

This kiln is a workhorse that is built to last and it simply plugs into standard 120volt - 15amp outlet to achieve 1700°F (927°C). It includes a pre-programmed digital controller, leaving you to choose only the firing speed (slow, medium or fast) and the process (slump, tack-fuse or full-fuse). That's it - 2 choices and the kiln is ready to fire. Or, use simple manual overrides to set your own process times and temperatures.

• Firing Chamber Dimensions: 14.5" diameter x 6.5" deep (37 cm diameter x 16.5 cm deep)

http://www.system96.com/

Skutt - GM22CS

This "Clamshell Kiln" was conceived to be a versatile kiln for glass fusing artists. The spring-shock supported lid opens from the bottom to provide unencumbered access to the spacious firing chamber. The integrated GlassMaster digital controller has convenient single button controls with an 8-segment program. It requires a dedicated 220volt - 30amp electrical hookup.

• Firing Chamber Dimensions: 22" square x 12" deep (56 cm diameter x 30.5 cm deep)

http://www.skutt.com/

Kiln Shelves:

The most common shelf used for glass fusing is the traditional clay kiln shelf made from Mullite clay. These shelves are available from all kiln supply distributors and are usually an inch or two (2.5 to 5 cm) smaller then the inside dimension of the kiln itself. In larger kilns clay shelves are often raised off the floor on 1/2" high kiln posts to allow heat to circulate. A raised shelf is also easier to remove, especially larger shelves that can be quite heavy.

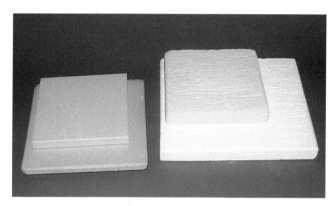

A standard Mullite clay kiln shelf (left) and one made using alumina silica 'fiberboard' material. Both are effective but the 'fiberboard' shelf has several key advantages (see text below).

Alternate Shelf Material:

A relatively new material that is gaining popularity among fusers is made from alumina silica 'fiberboard'. This material is lightweight and due to its insulating value it does not retain heat and therefore can be placed directly on the kiln floor. In addition, bubbles caused by trapped air under the glass during fusing is less likely to occur due to the porous nature of this material. Kaiser-Lee™ Board is one brand of fiberboard that is ready to use immediately. Other brands, such as Duraboard™ and Fiberfrax™, require some pre-use preparation such as a 'burnout' firing to release the organic binders and/or the application of a hardening material. Fiberboard has many advantages over traditional clay shelves, be sure to ask your fusing supplier for details on the brand they carry.

Kiln Posts:

Mullite clay posts are available in an assortment of heights and are used to raise clay shelves off the kiln floor plus they are used to support and raise molds when deep slumping (see page 10 top right).

Molds:

Glass forming molds are essential components for glass fusing. The expression "kiln formed glass" refers to glass that was formed to a certain shape using a mold in a kiln. A mold can be made from nearly any material that can withstand glass-forming temperatures.

Molds for glass forming can be made from:

- Bisque Fired Ceramic, formed clay shapes
- Stainless Steel, formed sheet metal
- Refractory Fire Brick, for carving
- Refractory Casting Material, for molding
- Ceramic Fiber Products in the form of:
  - Fiber Paper - 1/8" (3.2mm) & 1/32" (0.8mm) soft, flexible hi-temp material
  - Fiber Blanket - 1/2" (13mm) & 1" (25mm) soft fluffy 'blanket-like', hi-temp material
  - Fiberboard - rigid board, soft porous, easy to cut & shape, available in thicknesses of: 1/2", 1", 1 1/2", & 2" (13, 25, 38, & 51mm)

These shapes were all cut from a single 7" x 9" (18 x 23 cm) piece of fiberboard material. These assorted shapes can be used to create a variety of interesting projects. These mold items will be used several times to kiln-form projects in this book.

Of course there are proprietary brands, size & thickness variations, hardener & rigidizer treatments among other unique features within each category.

Glass forming introduces an additional level of difficulty into the fusing process and for this reason we will concentrate our instruction on using basic mold shapes and materials. I think you will be pleasantly surprised how much can be accomplished.

Glass For Fusing

The critical consideration when purchasing glass for fusing is compatibility. In glass fusing terminology, 'fusing compatible glass' means that two or more different pieces of glass can be melted together and when cooled are free from stress. Fused items that have internal stresses are susceptible to spontaneous cracking or breaking. This has been known to happen a year or more after the piece is finished.

Tested compatible art glass is available in many combinations. Left is a 2 color streaky and right are single color cathedrals.

This stress is introduced during the heating and cooling cycles and is the result of two distinct dynamics. Glass expands upon heating and contracts upon cooling. To be considered 'compatible for fusing' glass must expand and contract (extension & reduction of area) at a similar rate throughout the firing cycle. In addition the viscosity characteristics (resistance to flow) of 'fusing compatible' glass must also harmonize. If one glass is more rigid than the other stress will be introduced as they cool through the annealing range. Both of these compatibility issues must be factored in before a glass can be designated as 'fusing compatible'.

Fortunately manufacturers of fusible glass have taken on the responsibility for testing and offer glass that has been 'pre-tested' to be compatible. A 'tested compatible' glass is assigned a 'COE' number that represents the 'coefficient of expansion'. It is OK to use glass from different manufacturers in the same project, provided the COE number is the same.

As you might expect 'tested compatible' glass is slightly more expensive than standard art glass, but it is well worth it. Of course all glass manufacturers issue a disclaimer that recommends further testing the glass for compatibility. For most fusing work I leave the testing to the professionals and I have rarely encountered a problem (the few times I've had a problem can be traced to a glass mix-up within my own studio). However, I might recommend additional testing if you were fabricating a complicated project or one that required a substantial investment in fusible glass.

Be sure to purchase glass that you know is tested compatible. When buying full-sheet glass it should have a special sticker right on the glass (see samples of these stickers in photo below) that designates it as fusible glass. If you're buying smaller cut-up sheets make sure you're purchasing them from a reliable source, to be confident that the glass is the classification of 'tested compatible' that the supplier says it is.

These are typical examples of 'tested compatible' glass stickers. Be sure to check for these when buying glass for fusing.

Tested compatible glass has other advantages as well. There is less risk of devitrification (a term used to describe when glass loses its shiny luster and transparency). In addition tested compatible glass with an iridescent coating is less likely to fade during firing. Glass manufacturers provide a wealth of technical information on their particular glass that is invaluable when calculating a firing schedule.

Tested Compatible Glass Manufacturers

Currently four companies are manufacturing glass that is pre-tested for compatibility with two distinctly different COE designations. Both COE lines have extensive selections of colors and textures to choose from and all techniques in this book are appropriate for either one.

- Bullseye Glass Co. produces a line of 'tested compatible' with a COE 90 - www.bullseye-glass.com/
- Spectrum Glass Co. offers a range of pre-tested 'System 96' glass with a COE 96 - www.spectrumglass.com/
- Uroboros Glass Studios has two separate pre-tested lines, one in the 'System 96' style and the other is 'tested compatible' with a COE 90 - www.uroboros.com/
- Wasser Glass Co. manufactures a variety of 'tested compatible' with a COE 90 - www.dticrafts.com/

Clearly these two different COE lines of glass (COE 90 & COE 96) are not compatible with one another. I like to use both lines in my studio, but it is a challenge to keep them separated from each other.

Note: There are other glass manufacturers with glass classified for fusing. Some have vastly different COE designations so be sure to carefully check for this whenever you're purchasing glass for fusing.

HotTip

It is crucial to keep COE 90 and COE 96 glass distinctly separated. If you get these different COE glasses mixed up within the same project, you will most certainly have a disappointment when you open your kiln after firing. One effective method is to use color-coded small dot stickers (available from any office supply store). Place a blue dot (or any color you like) on all COE 90 glass and red dots on COE 96 (or you could use a permanent marker to add a special code). Whenever you cut a larger sheet into smaller pieces, place the correct color dot code onto each and every leftover piece before storing them. For smaller pieces set up scrap bins with the COE number on them and then place scraps into the correct bin.

Glass Types:

Within each of the COE categories of glass you will find an assortment of types and styles. Art glass (a.k.a. stained glass) is available in a wide variety of colors, textures and surface coatings. The main categories are clear glass (no color), cathedral glass (transparent colors), and opalescent glass (translucent colors). Glass in each of these categories can be further enhanced with surface textures and coatings. Iridescent glass has a thin coating of metallic chloride solution that produces subtle rainbow-like colors reflected by light. Dichroic Glass is a recent development that also has a metallic-look surface but Dichroic has a vivid range of color and a captivating intensity that can turn an ordinary project into an absolute work of art all by itself.

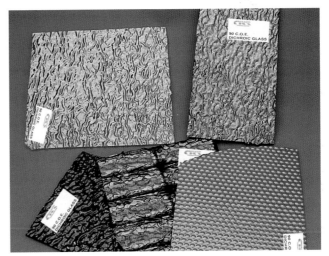

This photo shows 5 different samples of dichroic glass. The base glass in each of these is solid black, however each one has an entirely different texture & dichroic color combination.

Fusible glass is most commonly formed into sheets, but it can also be produced in other formats that are very useful. For example, stringers are long thin threads of glass (similar to spaghetti or angel hair pasta); noodles are thin and flat (similar to a linguine noodle). Glass frit is small pieces of crushed glass sorted and graded into sizes from 1/16" to 1/4" (1.6 to 6.4 mm), powder is finely crushed colored glass (the consistency of sugar), shards are paper thin glass pieces, and billets are 8" x 12" (20.3 x 30.5 cm) solid glass blocks approximately 3/4" (2 cm) thick.

Examples of the 'Tested Compatible' stickers on fusible glass.

CHAPTER SEVEN

Glass Scoring & Breaking

Not surprisingly the first thing you will need is a glasscutter. You can find very inexpensive cutters on the market but this is one of those instances where you get what you pay for. I recommend only the professional style cutters with a high quality carbide-steel cutting wheel. Most of these cutters have an oil reservoir with an automatic oil feeding system so the choice comes down to the cutter style that feels most comfortable in your hand. The best thing to do is try a few different cutter styles until you find one that works for you (your glass retailer will be happy to let you 'try a few on' for size).

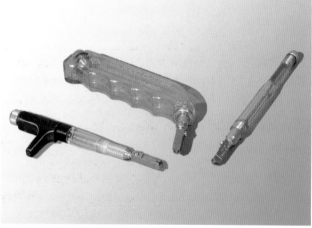

A selection of glass cutters, each one has the same professional scoring head, the difference is the shape and style of the handle.

Safety Considerations

Let's start with some rules for handling glass safely:

• Use safety gloves when handling large glass sheets.

• Always carry sheet glass in a vertical position. Never pick it up or move it in a horizontal (flat) position. The correct way to pick up and carry a glass sheet is to grasp it with both hands by the top edge or, for a larger (heavier) sheet, pick it up with one hand on the top edge and the other hand supporting the weight on the bottom edge.

• Never run your hand along a glass edge. Always release your grip to move your hand to a new position.

• Always wear safety glasses to protect your eyes while scoring and breaking.

Always carry sheet glass in a vertical position. The correct way to pick up and carry a glass sheet is to grasp it with both hands by the top edge.

Scoring and Breaking

It is a good idea to begin your practice cutting on standard clear glass (1/8" - 3mm window glass). This glass is inexpensive and is more forgiving for your first attempts at scoring and breaking. You will have a chance to get familiar with your tools, establish the proper cutter scoring pressure and learn the basic score breaking skills. Try shorter length scores at first, as they are generally easier to break out. Continue to practice on this glass until you get the feel for scoring and breaking. For greater stability and a better line of sight, you should be standing in a comfortable position with your work directly in front of you and wear those safety glasses while scoring and breaking.

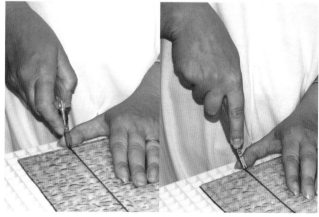

Two different ways to hold a glass cutter. There are actually many correct ways to hold a cutter, if you discover a way that is comfortable and works for you - then it's correct!

Introduction to Glass Fusing

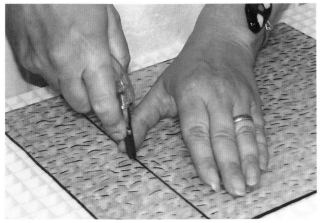

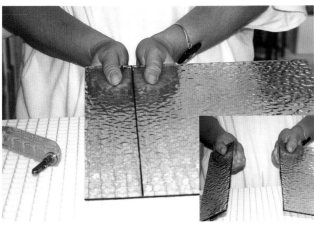

Making the Score

Hold the cutter in your favored (tool) hand and place the cutter wheel on the glass as close to the edge as possible. Now, place the thumb of your other (guide) hand behind the cutter head to prevent it from rolling back off the glass edge (see photo opposite page, bottom right). Apply a firm, constant pressure straight down onto the cutter with your tool hand and push it away from you with your guide hand. Score all the way across the surface of the glass and let the cutter wheel roll gently off the far edge.

ProTip: Take a moment to observe your score, it should appear as a clean, even, faint white line. If there are small glass chips popping from the score line, or if it appears gritty, then you have exerted too much pressure on the cutter. If you can hardly see the score then you didn't apply enough pressure (this is the most common problem for beginners).

Breaking Out The Score

After making a score you need to run or 'break out' the score. The break will start at one end of the score line and run (follow) along the score to the other side.

Breaking with hands only: Form both hands into fists and place the glass between your thumbs and index fingers with the score line between your thumbs. Your fingers should be clenched underneath the glass with knuckles touching. Hold the glass firmly at the end of the score (see 2nd down photo at left). Begin the break by pulling outward, then apply a quick even snap by spreading your thumbs apart, rolling on your knuckles. The glass should snap as your hands impulsively move apart (see inset left).

Breaking with the Morton "Button & Bar": Place the score over the button about 2" (5 cm) in from the glass edge. Now place the bar on the glass, centered over the button and aligned with the score. Press down with a firm but gentle pressure. If the score doesn't break right away, position the glass a bit further along over the button and press down again, repeat moving and pressing until the score breaks.

Breaking with Running Pliers: Align the guide mark on the top jaw of the running pliers with the score line about 3/8" (1cm) in from the glass edge. Gently squeeze the pliers until the break runs along the score line. If the break travels only part way along the score, simply move the breaking pliers to the opposite end of the score and repeat.

Project 1 - Tangram Puzzle

This is one of my favorite project designs. I've made dozens of these in many color combinations. A Tangram is an ancient Chinese puzzle-game. The object of this game is to rearrange the seven geometric pieces to a variety of shapes and forms. You can play it solitaire or with family and friends. You'll find some puzzle pictograms on page 24 and the solutions for them on page 78.

What You'll Learn

- Glass cutting shapes to a pattern
- Preparing the glass for firing
- Using Thinfire™ paper on a kiln shelf
- Assembling glass components on a shelf for firing
- First firing of a kiln
- Compare double layer firing with single layer

Tools & Equipment

- Glass cutting tools
- Permanent marker
- Scissors (for cutting fiber paper)
- Glass cleaning supplies
- Kiln, kiln controller and kiln shelf

Materials

- Glass - either COE 90 or COE System 96:

    - 4" x 4" (10.2 x 10.2 cm) or larger, clear cathedral

    - 4" x 4" (10.2 x 10.2 cm) or larger, dark blue cathedral

Note about glass choice: The process is the same for COE 90 or COE System 96 glass so the choice of glass is yours. However it is important that all glass used in any individual project has the same COE number.

- Thinfire™ paper; 2 pcs. - 5" x 5" (13 x 13 cm) or just large enough to cover your kiln shelf
- Tangram Pattern (on following page)

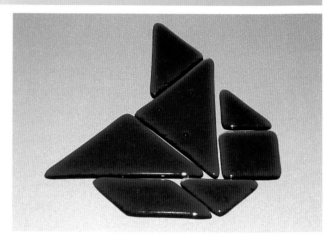

A Note About The Projects In This Book.

Every craft has its own set of unique words and definitions and this is also true for glass fusing. As you read through this book you'll become familiar with the distinctive vocabulary without realizing it. Project instructions are presented in a step-by-step format and include firing schedules and the material used.

Feel free to add your own flair to any of the projects but please stay close to the physical sizes and numbers of layers as specified in the project until you understand how changes would affect the firing schedule.

Step-by-Step Instructions

See page 18 & 19 for the basic scoring and breaking techniques that we will use for this project. Make sure your glass is free of dust and dirt and that it lays flat on your cutting surface. Art glass often has a smooth side and a rough side and it is generally easier to score on the smoother side. Hold the glass at an angle in the light and observe both sides, or run your hand over the surfaces to determine the smoothest side then lay the glass smooth side up on your table.

1. The first step is to cut two 4" (10.2 cm) squares, one from the clear and one from the blue glass. Start with the clear glass and draw the square on the glass. The easiest way is to place the glass on top of the pattern. If you have a square corner on the glass sheet place that corner on a corner of the pattern and use a ruler and a felt marker to transfer the remaining outside lines. Make sure to extend one of the lines from one side of the glass sheet to the other (see red line in Illustration A).

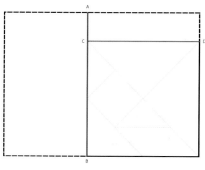

Illustration A

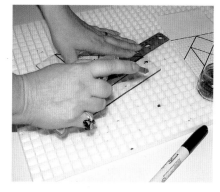

2. Make your first score from point A to point B (the red line in illustration A) and immediately break that score. You could break it using the hand method, the running pliers, or the Morton system. Use the method that you found to be most successful during your scoring and breaking practice, see page 19.

3. The second score will be from point C to point D (see blue line in Illustration A) and immediately break out that score using your preferred breaking method.

4. Repeat this procedure for the blue glass. You should now have two 4" (10.2 cm) square pieces; one from clear and one from blue.

5. Next we will cut each of these squares into the 7 geometrical Tangram pieces. The easiest way to transfer the pattern is to place the glass on top of the pattern, Illustration B below left, and use a ruler and a felt marker to transfer the lines. Your glass should have the same lines as the photo above.

6. The following two illustrations (B and C below) demonstrate the proper cutting and breaking sequence. It is important to follow this order (using the letters as indicated in illustration B) to correctly segment the Tangram puzzle pieces.

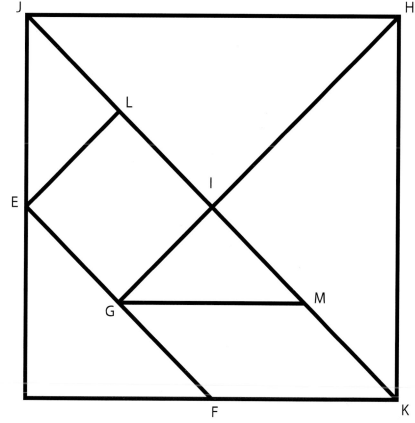

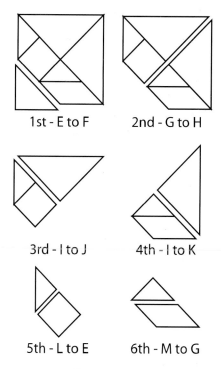

1st - E to F

2nd - G to H

3rd - I to J

4th - I to K

5th - L to E

6th - M to G

Illustration C

Illustration B - To correctly segment the Tangram puzzle pieces, use the letters in the illustration above to score and break the glass in the following order: 1st - E to F; 2nd - G to H; 3rd - I to J; 4th - I to K; 5th - L to E; 6th - M to G. Remember to break out the score immediately, *do not make all the scores* first and then try to break the glass.

7. When all pieces have been cut, it is very important that you clean the glass thoroughly before firing. The glass must be free of marker inks, cutting oil, and fingerprints. Otherwise these impurities could be fired into the glass and leave a permanent stain. Remove the marker lines using rubbing alcohol, and then wash the pieces in warm water with a little dish detergent. Dry them fully with a clean towel.

8. Stack the matching shaped glass pieces of clear and blue on top of each other. You can stack them with the clear glass on top / blue on the bottom or the inverse. Putting the clear glass on top will give the fused piece more depth and shine. Blue glass on top / clear on the bottom will give the pieces a more solid appearance. If you place the rough side of the clear glass against the rough side of the blue glass you will most likely find little bubbles trapped between the glass layers after fusing. It is good to remember this tendency and use it to create interesting design elements in your pieces (e.g. when simulating marine life).

HotTip

Never put wet or even damp components in your kiln, including the kiln shelf, prior to firing. Even a small amount of dampness will produce steam and that can easily cause the glass to blow-up!

Single layer of glass

Double layer of glass

HotTip

Why do we need two layers of glass anyway? The simple fact is glass changes shape during firing. If we tried to fire polish the edges of these puzzle pieces as a single layer only, the geometrical shape would be altered too much and the puzzle would be un-useable. The photo above left, shows the result of a puzzle that was fired with only a single layer of blue glass. However, when two layers of glass are stacked and taken to full fuse (photo above right) they hold their shapes very nicely.

9. Mullite clay shelves must have a separator material placed between the shelf and the glass or the molten glass will stick to the shelf during firing. Two main types of separators are kiln shelf wash (a.k.a. primer) and Thinfire™ shelf paper. Shelf wash can be sprinkled dry onto the shelf but more often it is mixed with water and painted onto the shelf, then left to dry prior to firing. Kiln wash is a popular separator material used by many fusers and we have a project that will cover it in detail a little later (see page 35).

10. For this project we will use a quick and easy separator material called 'Thinfire™' paper. Use scissors to cut two pieces of Thinfire™ paper approximately 5" X 5" (13 x 13 cm) or slightly smaller than the size of your kiln shelf. Place one of the Thinfire™ papers on your kiln shelf (the other will be used for the second firing).

11. Now we need to assemble and place the stacked glass components on the Thinfire™ paper covered shelf. Since we're using our small kiln for this project there is not enough room for all components to fit on one shelf and this means we will have to do two separate firings. Place the glass pieces on the kiln shelf, leaving a minimum of 1/2" (13 mm) space between them to ensure they do not touch and fuse together.

12. Place the kiln shelf (with your glass components arranged on it) on the kiln floor and fire the kiln according to the steps presented in the next section 'The Kiln Firing Process' on page 25 using the firing chart for Small Components - Full Fuse - 2 Layers.

HotTip

Thinfire™ Paper, Fiber Paper and Fiberboard are 3 distinctly different products that are often confused.

Thinfire™ Shelf Paper is 1/32" (0.8 mm) 'paper-thin' ceramic paper that is used as a shelf or mold separator. When fired this material disintegrates into dust and is easily brushed or washed off the fired glass leaving a smooth matt finish.

Fiber Paper comes in 1/32" (0.8 mm) and 1/8" (4 mm) thicknesses. This material can also be used as a shelf separator that leaves a stippled finish on the glass. We often use the 1/8" (4 mm) paper to create open loops (pg 15), reverse indents (pg 15) or basic molds (pg 15). This material contains an organic binder that produces a pungent odor as it burns off.

Fiberboard is a thick rigid material available in thicknesses of: 1/2", 1", 1 1/2", & 2" (13, 25, 38, & 51mm). Fiberboard can be used in place of a kiln shelf and is easily cut and carved into custom glass-forming molds. For more information refer to 'Alternate Shelf Material ' on page 15.

13. After the kiln has cooled to room temperature open or remove the lid of the kiln and set it aside. Wash the Thinfire™ paper from the glass using a wet paper towel. Be careful to avoid breathing the dust from the Thinfire™ paper and do not use your sink to wash it off because it can clog your water drain.

14. Now that you have one successful firing under your belt finish the remaining puzzle pieces with a second firing by repeating steps 7 through 13.

15. Congratulations, you have finished your first fused glass project and it's time to have fun with the puzzle you've created. The 3 photos below and the illustrations at the bottom of the page are examples of figures that you can create with these Tangram pieces. It's not as easy as it looks, see if you can figure out how they were made.

ProTip: The parallelogram (diamond) shaped piece is sometimes used upside down! You may want to make an additional puzzle piece in this configuration.

The Internet is a great resource for even more Tangram figures to solve. In fact, there is a site that is dedicated entirely to the Tangram puzzle. Be sure to check out http://www. tangrams. ca/

HotTip

The presentation frame shown in the photos below were created by fastening a piece of galvanized sheet metal to a plywood base and painting it with metallic spray paint (auto touch-up paint). Then we glued magnetic sheets (available from any craft supply store) to the backside of the Tangram glass pieces so they could be moved around and rearranged on the sheet metal frame. This frame completes the project and makes a great hostess gift for a party, but make sure to include some of the unsolved silhouettes to make the game interesting.

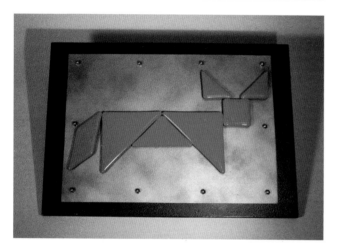
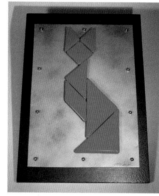

These Tangram pictograms are not as easy to solve as they look. Try your hand at them and when you give up turn to page 78.

Introduction to Glass Fusing

Tutorial - The Kiln Firing Process - Using a Smaller Kiln

This 'Small Component' Fuse-firing Technique is appropriate for any project that is 4 square inches (25 sq-cm) or smaller. The steps will cover kilns that have manual control switches. If your kiln has an automatic digital controller, all you'll need to do is set it for a 'fast, full-fuse firing' and turn it on. However, you should still read this section to find out what is actually happening during the automatic fusing cycle.

It is amazing how many different kinds of projects you can make in a smaller kiln. They are ideal for learning the basics of glass fusing. Since they heat up so quickly, advanced fusers love them for experimentation and testing. The kilns we used for the photos in this section are the QuikFire 6 kiln by Paragon and the HotBox kiln by Evenheat (see pages 12 to 14 for more entry-level kilns).

We will show this Quickfire 6 kiln and the Evenheat Hotbox in this fuse-firing demonstration, however the process would be the same for any model of smaller kiln.

HotTip

It is usually not a good idea to use an extension cord with any kiln. These may be small kilns but the power draw is substantial and a standard-duty extension cord will heat up quickly and become a serious fire hazard. There are heavy-duty extension cords available that may work, but the easiest and best solution by far is to put the kiln close enough to an outlet.

What You'll Learn

- Full-fuse firing technique
- How to read a firing chart
- How to Calculate a Temperature 'Ramp Rate'

Tools & Equipment

- Kiln with pyrometer or digital controller
- Tangram puzzle (or any small full-fuse project)
- Kiln shelf, with primer or Thinfire™ paper
- High temp kiln gloves
- Kitchen minute timer
- Safety glasses, goggles or other eye protection

Step-by-Step Instructions

1. Set your kiln on a sturdy bench, preferably one that is non-flammable and close enough to reach a convenient outlet without using an extension cord (see HotTip below left). Make sure to keep it a good distance away from anything that may be flammable.

2. Most small kilns operate on a standard household 120V-15A circuit, and that means all you have to do is plug it in. However, some kilns have a controller that plugs into the power outlet and the kiln plugs into the controller. Be sure to read the directions and warnings that came with your kiln before you turn it on for the first time.

3. Cut, clean and assemble your glass components, prepare the kiln shelf and position your fusing project on the shelf according to the project directions. If you have placed multiple items on the same shelf remember to leave at least 1/2" (13 mm) in between.

What is considered a 'Small Component'?

Any project that is 4 square inches (25 sq-cm) or smaller. To calculate the square area simply multiply the height x width (i.e. 2.5" x 2" = 5 sq-in (6 x 5 cm = 33 sq-cm). The largest individual component in the Tangram Puzzle is a triangle that is 2" x 4" (5 x 10 cm) that equals 4 sq-in (25 sq-cm). We could successfully fire as many items as our kiln shelf could hold, provided they were this size or smaller.

4. Depending on the type of kiln you have either remove the top section of the kiln from the bottom part or take the top-cover off or open the hinged lid (it's up to you to figure out which one applies to your kiln). Place the kiln shelf (with your glass components arranged on it) on the kiln floor. Make a final check of your glass to make sure they are aligned and separated then carefully replace the lid section. Make sure the top is positioned correctly and be careful not to shake your pieces apart.

5. I like to vent the kiln by placing a small piece of fiberboard or brick under the front side of the lid to lift it about 1/2" (13 mm). This allows the fumes created by the shelf paper and/or glue to escape from the kiln. Otherwise these fumes can leave a stain on the surface of the glass.

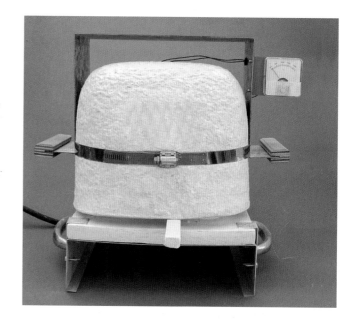

SMALL COMPONENTS - FULL FUSE - 2 LAYERS

Phase	Temp/Min	Arrive Temp	SoakTime	Action
Temp Up	30°F / 18°C	1000°F / 535°C	1 min	Remove Vent
Temp Up	Full-speed	*1500°F / 815°C	10+/- min	Observe
Flash Cool	High-speed	1100°F / 590°C	0 min	Open & Close Lid
Temp Hold	5°F / 3°C	955°F / 513°C	10 min	Hold your fire
Cool Down	Undisturbed	100°F / 38°C	N/A	Do Not Peek

* 'Arrive' Temperature will vary; it is essential to 'Observe' your project carefully as it approaches.

HotTip

Temp/Min is the 'Temperature change per Minute' and describes the speed of the heating cycle. This is an important measurement in kiln-fired glass and you will need this number for both manual and automatic controllers. Here's how to calculate the Temp/Min. Let's assume the start temperature of a kiln is 75°F (24°C) we turn it on medium, check it after 30 minutes and the temp has reached 675°F (357°C). We have 'ramped-up' at 20°F (12°C) per minute. Here's how you figure that out using simple math (and a calculator). Current temp, minus starting temp, divided by minutes elapsed, equals temp/min. One more example; start temp is 500°F (260°C) after 15 minutes the current temp is 775°F (413°C). So, 775°F (413°C) minus 500°F (260°C) divided by 15 is 18.3°F (10.2°C) temp/min. It's that simple!

6. Most fusers use firing charts to guide them through the firing procedure. This chart is typical of the style we will use for the projects in this book to specify the firing procedure. Let's take a look at this chart, describe how to read it and how to implement the steps.

7. The title of this chart, 'Small Components - Full Fuse - 2 Layers' identifies the parameters for this firing schedule. Use it if the glass components are 2" x 2" (5 x 5 cm) or smaller (see page 25 bottom right), going to full-fuse stage (totally merged), with 2 layers of glass. Not coincidentally this describes our Tangram project exactly.

8. The headings across the top of the chart describe the stages for each step. 'Phase' is what the kiln should be doing; 'Temp/Min' is the 'Temperature change per Minute' (see HotTip left); 'Arrive Temp' is the temperature that we're looking to reach; 'Soak Time' is how long you want to hold the kiln at the Arrive Temp before moving to the final; 'Action' step for something that you must do - or not do - as the case may be.

The subsequent rows are the steps that you need to follow to complete the firing. We will take a look at each one in detail as we go through the steps to fuse-fire this Tangram project.

9. OK enough theory - Let's get fired up! The first row of the firing chart is *'Temp Up'* and it tells us that we need to achieve a 30°F (18°C) per minute ramp rate so let's turn the manual kiln controller to the number 2 position and set the kitchen timer for 15 minutes. When the timer alarm sounds check the temperature and calculate the temp/min to make sure it is close to the recommended rate in the firing chart (see HotTip on Page 26). At 30°F (18°C) per minute the kiln should be somewhere around 525°F (275°C) after 15 minutes. If the temperature is lower that's OK but it shouldn't be too much higher. If it is, you may want to make a note for next time, to start your kiln at a lower setting for a few minutes before turning it up to to a higher power position.

10. Now set the controller to position 3 and the timer for another 15 minutes. When the alarm sounds again (now 30 minutes from the start) check the temperature and if it has reached 1000 °F (535°C) proceed to step 11. If the temperature has not quite reached 1000 °F (535°C) turn the controller to position 4 and stay with the kiln until it does get to 1000 °F (535°C). If it has gone past 1000 °F (535°C) don't panic, just make a note to keep your controller turned down a bit when you do your next firing.

The temperature has reached fuse level and it's important to keep checking until you can see that the original 2 layers of glass have fully merged into a single layer. Note: this photo shows the Quickfire 6 kiln.

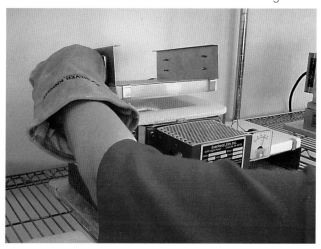

Lift the lid carefully to remove the venting block. This photo shows the Evenheat Hotbox kiln.

11. Once the kiln is at 1000 °F (535°C) let it soak there for a minute or so then put on your hi-temp gloves, remove the venting block and close the lid. Do not be tempted to open the lid all the way to take a long peek because the cold air could cause a thermal shock and shatter your glass. While you're waiting, do your Temp/Min calculation for future reference.

12. The 1st row of the firing chart is complete. The 2nd row Phase is still *'Temp Up'* but the Temp/Min says *'Full-speed'* indicating that the kiln can ramp up from here as fast as it can go. So, let's turn the controller to maximum and stay with the kiln.

13. It won't take long to reach 1500°F (815°C). When it does. put your hi-temp gloves back on and your safety glasses (to protect your eyes from the radiant heat) and lift the lid, just a little bit, so you can see the glass. It likely won't be fully fused yet but you will be able to clearly see that the glass has started to melt and combine and it will give you a starting reference point.

14. Close the lid and wait a little while before taking another look - the chart says the 'soak time' is 10+/- minutes. During this time your kiln will continue to heat up and the pyrometer will read anywhere between 1600°F (870°C) and 1800°F (980°C) before the glass is fully fused, see hot tip on page 28. This is why it is important to keep checking visually until the desired effect is achieved. Some kilns have a viewing window in the lid or in the side that offers a constant view of your work without having to lift the lid. This is a handy feature and one that you may want to consider when evaluating kilns for purchase.

15. The 3rd row in the chart is the *'Flash Cool'* Phase. When you are satisfied with the result visually, turn the controller to the off position (if your kiln has a switch turn that off as well). Put on your hi-temp gloves and safety glasses and tilt the lid way back to vent the kiln until the temperature has dropped to 1100°F (590°C) - this will only take a few seconds - then close the lid again. If the temp goes back up to 1200°F (650°C), vent it back to 1100°F (590°C) then do not open the lid again. Depending on the kiln, it could take 20 minutes to 1 hour or more for it to cool down to 955°F (513°C) ready for the next phase.

16. The 4th row on the chart is the *'Temp Hold'* Phase that will allow the glass to anneal. Annealing is a very important step to relieve internal stress in the glass. Proper annealing requires holding the glass at a pre-determined temperature until it has equalized. For this project we need to hold the temperature between 950°F & 960°F (510°C & 516°C) for 10 minutes. You may need to turn the kiln back on to position 3 for a few minutes to achieve this. Truth is, it's not really critical to 'anneal soak' the small items we are firing in this project since it will take more than 10 minutes for the temperature to fall through the annealing range anyway but it is good practice to watch for the annealing temp range just to be safe.

17. The last row in the chart is the *'Cool Down'* Phase and this one is fairly easy. Just turn off the kiln and - here comes the hard part - do not open the lid until the kiln has reached room temperature. This will take a few hours.

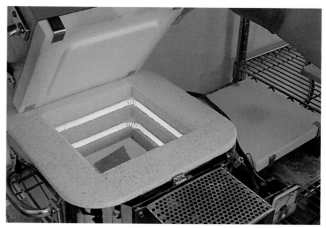

Put on your hi-temp gloves and safety glasses and tilt the lid back to vent the kiln until the temperature has dropped to 1100°F (590°C) - this will only take a few seconds.

HotTip

Why is a 'full-fuse' firing between 1600°F (870°C) and 1800°F (980°C) in these kilns, when the chart on page 7 says a full fuse is between 1450°F (790°C) and 1550°F (790°C)? The answer is they're both correct. Glass is at full fuse when the temperature of 'the glass' is around 1480°F (805°C). However, the pyrometer indicates the air temperature inside the kiln and not the glass temperature. Glass is a bad heat conductor and these small kilns heat up so quickly the glass can't 'keep up' with the air temperature. In bigger kilns the ramp up speed is usually much slower, allowing the glass time to achieve a temperature closer to the air inside the kiln.

The Cool Down phase is fairly easy, just turn off the kiln. The most difficult part is resisting the urge to open the lid before the kiln has reached room temperature.

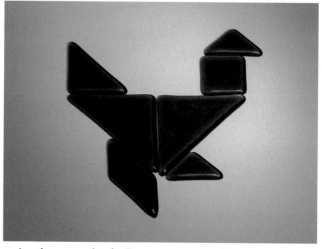

Another example of a Tangram creature - Fire Bird anyone?

Project 2 - Office Cubical Clock

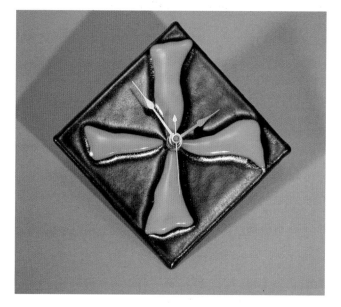

Sometimes I teach glass fusing at locations where I have to bring all the necessary equipment with me. Obviously I cannot take my large kilns so I had to come up with some interesting projects that students could make in the smaller and more portable kilns. I decided to create a simple square clock project. It fits nicely into the firing chamber of even the smallest kiln and it is a useful and creative item that also makes a great gift.

What You'll Learn

- Scoring and breaking curved lines
- Using a glass grinder
- Drilling a hole in glass

Tools & Equipment

- Glass cutting tools
- Permanent marker
- Scissors (for cutting fiber paper)
- Glass cleaning supplies
- Kiln, kiln controller and shelf
- Glass grinder with 1/4" (6.4 mm) bit attachment
- High-speed hand-held drill with 5/16" (8 mm) hollow-core diamond-coated glass drill bit
- Tray approximately 1/2" (13 mm) deep - with just enough water to submerge 2 layers of glass. A plastic 'cafeteria-style' tray works wonderfully

Materials

- Glass (either COE but all glass must be the same):
  - 5" x 5" (13 x 13 cm) dark blue, cath iridescent
  - 3" x 5" (8 x 13 cm) apple green, opalescent
- Clockworks (battery operated) with small hands
- 5 1/4" x 5 1/4" (14 x 14 cm) Thinfire™ paper
- Small piece of fiber paper
- White glue, for pre-firing assembly

Step-by-Step Instructions

1. Cut a 5" x 5" (13 x 13 cm) square piece from the dark blue iridescent glass. When you choose the type and color of glass for your clock, make sure to select something that will hide the clockworks.

The paper pattern is placed on the blue glass ready for tracing.

2. Now cut the design elements. For this project we will create 4 pinwheel shapes with simple curvy lines. Find the smoothest side of the glass and transfer your design by tracing with a permanent marking pen. Score the glass by following along the line. Break the glass using your breaker/grozer pliers, or use the Morton "button & bar" breaker system. Remember; always score completely across the glass from one edge to the other and break the glass after every score. Score and break all 4 of your design pieces.

3. Don't worry too much if the glass did not break exactly where you wanted it. As you can see in the photo at right, my shapes didn't exactly break out the way I had intended. The good news is you can often use the glass anyway, simply modify the design somewhat to make an allowance for the new shapes. Of course you could re-cut the pieces that didn't work, as they say "practice makes perfect" and this is as good a time as any to work on your scoring and breaking skills.

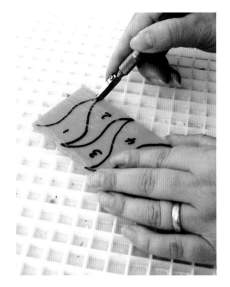
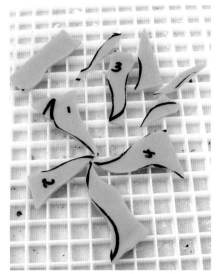

4. I've decided to use my glass grinder to rescue these poorly cut pieces (I wanted to show you how to use a grinder anyway). Before using your grinder always check the water level, make sure the sponge is wet and ensure it is functioning properly. Now put on your safety glasses, place your glass piece flat on the grinder table, turn the grinder on and gently push the glass into the spinning diamond bit. Don't push too hard. Let the grinder do the work by keeping a steady pressure while moving the glass from left to right. If you have a lot of grinding to do, you may want to wear rubber gloves or use grinder thumb-pushers to protect your hands. Grind the glass until you're satisfied with the shape of each piece.

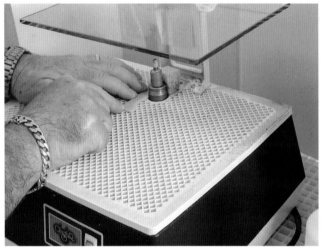

5. I prefer to remove the sharp corners on my blue base piece. Push the glass gently into the grinder bit, moving from left to right. Do this a couple of times to get a slightly rounded corner. You may wonder why you have to grind the corner since the kiln should round corners during fuse firing. The answer is that if we were firing two layers of glass the corners would round nicely but single layer fusing tends to leave corners more pointed.

ProTip: Try to be conservative with your grinding and grind only where it is absolutely necessary. As you might expect, grinding produces a roughened edge on the glass. Unfortunately this normally results in a murky discoloration of the edge after firing. This stain is less noticeable on light colored glass and may not be seen at all depending on where it is in the finished piece. It's not always a problem but it is something that you need to take into consideration when cutting and shaping your glass prior to firing.

6. When all the glass pieces are cut and shaped it's time to do the pre-firing assembly. Clean and dry all glass components. Cut a 1/4" (6 mm) circle of fiber paper and glue it to the backside (not the iridescent side) in dead center of your base glass. During firing this fiber paper disk will create a small indent that we will use as a guide to hold the drill bit in just the right place when drilling the center hole for the clock.

Introduction to Glass Fusing

7. Cover the kiln shelf with a piece of Thinfire™ paper and place the blue base glass, iridescent side up, on the paper. Next arrange your design pieces on top of the blue glass. When you are finished carefully place the shelf on the floor of the kiln.

Y ou may want to use a dab or two of white glue to hold the design elements in place on the background glass. This is especially helpful when the design is complex or when you're constructing several items at the same time. You can do all the assembly work and keep them on a 'ready to fire' shelf until the kiln is available for another firing.

8. Fire the kiln according to the steps presented in The Kiln Firing Process on page 25. Use the firing chart at right designed for Small/Med Components - Tack Fuse - 2 Layers. We fired our clock slightly more than a true tack fire but we didn't take it all the way to a full fuse. Watch your piece carefully when it is in the fuse temperature range and flash cool the kiln as soon as you are satisfied with the result.

SMALL/MED COMPONENTS - TACK FUSE - 2 LAYERS

Phase	Temp/Min	Arrive Temp	SoakTime	Action
Temp Up	15°F / 9°C	1000°F / 538°C	1 min	Remove Vent
Temp Up	Full-speed	*1350°F / 816°C	10+/- min	Observe
Flash Cool	High-speed	1100°F / 593°C	0 min	OpeN & Close Lid
Temp Hold	5°F / 3°C	955°F / 513°C	20 min	Hold your fire
Cool Down	Undisturbed	100°F / 38°C	N/A	Do Not Peek

* 'Arrive' Temperature will vary; it is essential to 'Observe' your project carefully as it approaches.

W e keep a plastic bucket filled with water in the kiln area of our studio that we call our 'dunk bucket'. It is nothing more than an office trash container, approximately 8″ x 14″ x 12″ deep (20 x 36 x 30 cm deep), filled with water and used to soak and wash the Thinfire™ paper off our fired pieces as soon as we've taken them from the kiln. Remember, you shouldn't wash the discarded Thinfire™ paper down the drain - it could create clogging problems later. The best method is to let the particles settle overnight and then carefully pour off the water leaving the particles in the bottom of the bucket. Place this fiber waste in a trash bag and discard.

9. When the kiln has cooled completely remove your fired piece and place it in the 'dunk bucket' (see HotTip at left) to wash off the Thinfire™ paper and discard the little circle of fiber paper.

10. Now we have to turn this fused square glass into a clock by drilling a hole in the center. We have two different methods for drilling this hole and we often use a combination of both methods to get the best-finished results.

11. The first method uses a high-speed portable drill (with a minimum 20,000 rpm) fitted with a 5/16" (8 mm) hollow-core diamond-coated glass drill bit (or sized to fit your clock part). It is best to drill the hole with the glass completely underwater. Use a shallow plastic tray (a cafeteria type tray) and lay a piece of 1/8" (3 mm) standard clear window glass in the bottom, then fill the tray with water.

ProTip: This 'tray-liner' glass is a little trick we learned from John and Addi de Pietro. It will stop the drill from going through the plastic tray but more importantly it inhibits strain fracturing of your fused piece. I could get into a big explanation as to how it works, but please just trust me - it works!

12. Ok here we go. Lay the fused clock face-side down (the fiber paper depression should be up) on the 'tray-liner' clear glass and make sure it is completely under water. Put on your safety glasses, hold the electric drill in a vertical position over the glass,

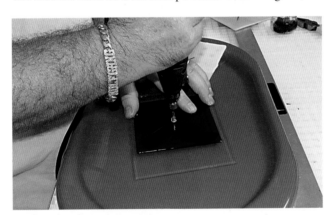

Here we are drilling the center hole in several different fired clock faces. Notice the selection of faces on the bench behind.

start the motor and slowly lower it into the fiber depression. Note: It is not necessary to have a depression to drill a hole, it is just a little more difficult to start the drilling without one. Try and resist the urge to hurry the drilling process by pressing down. You will find the weight of the drill - and some patience - is all that is necessary to cut through the glass. When the hole is drilled completely through, remove the glass from the water, dry it off and check to see if the hole is large enough to fit the clock shaft. If it's not quite big enough place the clock face back into the drilling tray and use the drill bit to ream it out slightly or the method I prefer to enlarge the hole is to use the drilling/grinding head on the grinder - see next step.

13. The alternate hole drilling method uses a glass grinder fitted with a 1/4" (6 mm) drilling/grinding head. The most important issue when drilling a hole with your grinder is to keep your glass and the grinder head wet. Use a sponge to drip water on the grinder head and on the glass (drip some in the little depression you made with the fiber paper circle). You must wear safety glasses for this operation - turn the glass upside down and lower it onto the spinning grinding head. Move the glass in a 'circular & back-and-forth' manner for 10 to 15 seconds. Then remove the glass from the grinder head and clean the residue out of the hole. Re-wet the head and continue grinding repeating this step until you have drilled completely through. Finally clean the glass and check the size of the hole. If it's not quite big enough put it back on the grinder bit (make sure it's wet) and move it around in a circular pattern until the hole is large enough.

14. The final step is to mount the clockworks. They usually come with their own instructions but it's a very simple and easy process. Then hang it up and have the 'Time' of your life.

Project 3 - Ceiling Fan or Window Shade Pull

The following project will introduce a fundamental assembly trick for an easy way to create a hanging loop for the top of this fan-pull, without having to drill a hole. This is an important basic technique that you will find useful to incorporate in a wide variety of applications. We have come to rely on it to create hanging loops in fused projects ranging from jewelry to wall sculptures.

Note: It's simple to adapt this same process to create an interesting key ring ornament or make an even smaller version to use as a necklace pendant.

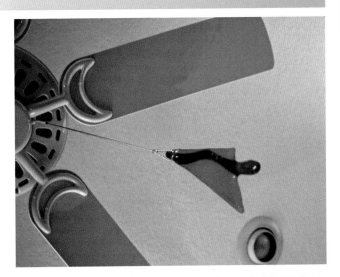

What You'll Learn

- A technique to create an open hanging loop without drilling a hole

- Fusing two different colors of cathedral glass to create a color shift

- Scoring and breaking narrow strips of glass

Tools & Equipment

- Glass cutting tools

- Permanent marker

- Scissors (for cutting fiber paper)

- Glass cleaning supplies

- Kiln, kiln controller and shelf

- Round nose jewelry pliers

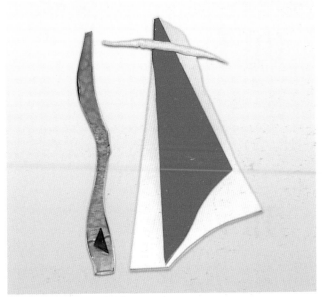

Materials

- Glass (either COE but all glass must be the same): as usual, the color choices are yours to make!

  - Small Piece - dark blue, cathedral iridescent

  - Small Piece - red, cathedral iridescent

- Thinfire™ paper, smaller scrap piece

- Fiber paper, small piece, (pre-fired/recycled OK)

- 12" (30 cm) bead chain and 2 connectors or cord depending on how you intend to use your pull.

Step-by-Step Instructions

1. Cut a triangle shaped base section from the red cathedral glass, to the size and shape you want. I made this one approximately 1.5" wide x 3" long (3.8 x 7.6 cm). Clean and dry this glass piece.

2. Cut a piece of Thinfire™ paper a little bigger than the size of your base glass piece and place it on the kiln shelf. Now you can put the red glass on the Thinfire™ paper.

3. Next cut a piece of 1/8" thick (3.2 cm) fiber paper, approximately 1/8" x 1" long (3.2 x 25 mm). Note: Fiber paper is a different product from the Thinfire™ paper - see HotTip on page 23.

4. Place the fiberpaper strip across the red base glass about 3/8" (9 mm), from the top.

5. Cut a tiny triangle of the red glass, or sort through the cutoff pieces you have to find an interesting shape that you can use as the decorative accent.

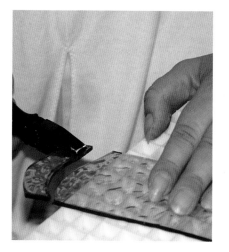
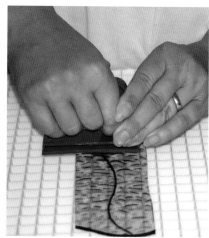

6. Next we need to cut a curvy strip from the blue cathedral glass. Score the glass and move it to the edge of your bench allowing the narrow piece to overhang slightly. Use the breaking pliers to grasp the glass strip at one end of the score. Pull out and away with the pliers then snap down. The curvy glass piece should easily break away from the larger glass piece.

ProTip: If you have a Morton glass workshop the 'button and block' breaker system is especially well suited to breaking out this type of score. Start the break at one end and move the glass across the button to continue the break along the score (see this device in action in the photo at top right).

7. Cut the blue wavy accent piece, clean it with rubbing alcohol and warm soapy water and dry.

8. Place the blue glass strip, on the red glass triangle and make sure it extends about 3/8" (9 mm) above the fiber paper strip. Finally place the little red triangle accent on the blue strip. We had to place a small Thinfire™ patch at the botttom for the blue glass.

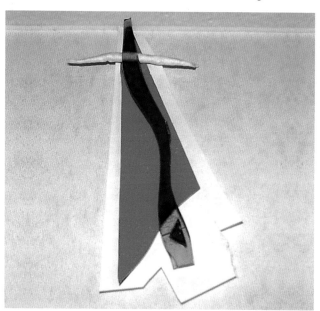

HotTip

Don't put the fiber paper strip too close to the top edge. As the glass heats up and bends it may not reach all the way around the strip to create a fully closed loop. However, you also have to be careful not to lay the fiber paper strip too far in the middle or your pull might not hang properly.

9. Place the kiln shelf (with your glass components arranged on it) on the kiln floor and fire the kiln according to the steps presented in 'The Kiln Firing Process' on page 25. Use the firing chart on page 26 designed for Small Components - Full Fuse - 2 Layers.

10. After the kiln has cooled to room temperature take your finished piece out and remove the old Thinfire™ paper using the dunk bucket, see HotTip on page 31. Be sure to carefully remove the fiber paper from inside the hanging loop - use a sharp stick.

ProTip: Take a moment to examine the color shift in the blue and the red glass. Sometimes you can predict how the color will change while other times it will not be what you expected.

11. Now we will finish the fan pull by installing the bead chain. Use the jewelry pliers to open one end of the connector and attach it to a bead about 2" from the end. Thread this end through the hanging loop in your glass pull and fasten the end bead through the other side of the connector. Hook the other end of the chain to a ceiling fan or a window shade.

Project 4 – Sunny Bells – Window Ornaments

This is another one of the projects we developed to make use of the smaller cut-off pieces of glass. Since you're just beginning to fuse you may not have a vast collection of scrap glass pieces yet but trust me you will, then you will find projects like this one invaluable.

What You'll Learn

- Using kiln wash to prepare a clay kiln shelf

Tools & Equipment

- Wide putty knife
- Hake brush and plastic mixing bowl
- Glass cutting tools
- Glass cleaning supplies
- Kiln, kiln controller and clay shelf

Materials

- Kiln shelf wash
- Small piece of fiber paper
- Glass - scrap pieces of COE 96 (or COE 90, the process is the same):

  - Assorted colors of cathedral and/or opal glass

1. - Two kinds of kiln wash
2. - Small kitchen strainer
3. - Nylon stocking filled with dry kiln wash
4. - Small plastic tray, to store the powder filled sock
5. - Mixing bowl
6. - Hake brush

Kiln Wash - a.k.a. Shelf Primer:

As we have learned, molten glass will stick to a clay shelf (or mold) unless a separator is placed between the glass and shelf. In the first 3 projects we used Thinfire™ paper as the separator and it is completely acceptable to use this product for all your projects, making kiln wash unnecessary. So why even bother with shelf primer? Well, that is how it has always been done and most fusers use kiln wash and clay shelves at least some of the time. Plus there are advantages to using kiln wash, for example it can give the shelf a very smooth surface, leaving the bottom of your fused piece with a minimum of texture. It is also inexpensive, as compared to Thinfire™ paper and it conforms easily to most high-fire surfaces, like curved or intricately shaped molds. Keep in mind you must allow 24 hours for the kiln wash to air dry before using. Traditional kiln wash has a tendency to stick to some glass types, especially opal colors and it can be tough to clean off but a relatively new and improved product is available. Primo Primer™ is applied to shelves and molds in the same way as a standard primer but is less likely to stick to fused glass and it turns to powder after being fired, making clean-up exceedingly easy.

Kiln wash can be used in dry form simply by sprinkling or sifting it onto the shelf or mold and we will use this method in a later project. The customary application method is to mix the powder with water and paint it (or spray it) onto the clay shelf or mold. I have stressed how important it is to dry your glass pieces prior to firing and it is even more imperative to ensure the shelf or molds are completely dry before you fire your glass on them. Firing glass on a shelf that is still damp will produce steam and steam will produce disaster!

Step-by-Step Instructions

1. The first step is to clean the shelf or mold of any previous pre-fired wash (if you're working with a new shelf or mold skip to step 2). I soak the shelf in water for a few minutes, scrape the shelf with a wide putty knife and finish by scrubbing with a stiff bristle brush. Finally run your hand lightly around the surface to feel for any bumps or ridges; if you find any make sure to clean them off as well.

2. Now we need to mix up a batch of wash. Most primers have the dilution instructions on the package and I suggest that you follow these directions if available. Otherwise I like to mix 1 part kiln wash in 5 parts of water (some fusers use a 1 to 4 ratio for a thicker mixture). Blend the mixture well but try to keep the bubbles to a minimum, as they will transfer to the shelf during application and then burst, creating a hollow spot.

> ### HotTip
>
> Shelf primer typically lasts for only one full-fuse high-temp firing. As a rule it should be cleaned off and reapplied after each use. There are times when a once-fired shelf can be re-fired however, it takes some experience to determine when a shelf can be safely re-used. We prefer to not take a risk with a used shelf, the time it takes to clean and re-prep a shelf is minor as compared to creating and firing a project only to have it stick to the shelf and be ruined.

3. Most fusers agree that a "hake" brush (used for Japanese watercolor painting) is the best choice to apply the kiln wash as they are soft and don't leave bristle marks. Load the brush and apply the first coat by painting it on first in one direction and then apply another coat at 90° to the first - apply about 4 to 6 thin layers alternating the direction each time. Finally let the shelf air dry for at least 24 hours.

4. Next we will prepare and assemble the glass components. Cut several pie shaped segments of glass from your collection of scrap glass. The pieces in my 'Sunny Bells' are approximately 4" long and 1" to 1-1/2" wide (10 x 2.5 to 3.8 cm). You could cut all the pieces from a single color or alternate from 2 colors or make each 'ray' a different color for a rainbow effect. Just make sure all the glass in the project has the same COE compatible number. You will also need a 3/4" (2 cm) square piece for the center.

5. You could get creative with the 3/4" (2 cm) square piece and cut the corners off to make an

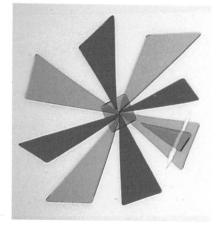

octagon. If you want you could even grind the octagon a little to make it into a circle. I like to round off the corners of the 'ray' triangles using my grinder. I think it gives the 'Sunny Bell' a softer look when finished. Remember to always wear your safety glasses while grinding.

6. Finally cut a piece of 1/8" thick (3.2 cm) fiber paper 1/8" x 1" long (3.2 x 25 mm). We're going to use it to create a hanging loop as we did in the 'Fan Pull' project, on page 33.

Introduction to Glass Fusing

7. Carefully clean and dry each glass component. Here we have them arranged on a tray to see how they will look then we will transfer them to our prepared kiln shelf. Remember to place the fiber paper strip across one of the rays and overlay it with a small piece of the same glass to create the hanging loop.

8. Place the shelf in your kiln, take one last look to make sure the glass components are exactly where they should be (fix any that are not) and fire it according to the steps presented in The Kiln Firing Process on page 25 - using the firing schedule below left for 'Full Fuse - 2 Layers'.

SMALL/MED COMPONENTS - FULL FUSE - 2 LAYERS

Phase	Temp/Min	Arrive Temp	SoakTime	Action
Temp Up	15°F / 9°C	1000°F / 538°C	1 min	Remove Vent
Temp Up	Full-speed	*1480°F / 805°C	10+/- min	Observe
Flash Cool	High-speed	1100°F / 593°C	0 min	Open & Close Lid
Temp Hold	5°F / 3°C	955°F / 513°C	15 min	Hold your fire
Cool Down	Undisturbed	100°F / 38°C	N/A	Do Not Peek

* 'Arrive' Temperature will vary; it is essential to 'Observe' your project carefully as it approaches.

9. After the kiln has cooled to room temperature take out your finished piece. Be sure to remove the fiber paper from inside the hanging loop, you may need something long and narrow to poke it through.

10. Finish the project by threading fishing line or a decorative cord through the hanging loop then place your 'Sunny Bell' in a window and enjoy.

These mobiles were created using a process very similar to the Sunny Bells project. We used up a lot of small scrap glass and created a movable sculpture to hang in a window.

Start by laying out a square frame using clear glass then add the color highlights as a second layer. The holes were created using the same fiber paper technique that we used to make the Sunny Bells hanging loop.

A long threaded bolt was used for the final assembly. These are available from most hardware stores. You might want to locate this part first to determine the maximum height that your mobile can be.

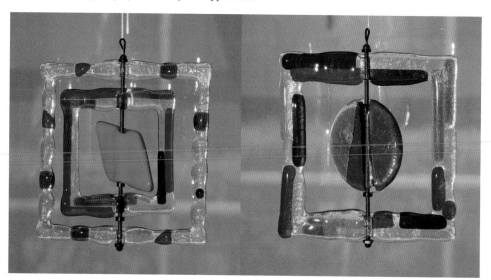

Introduction to Glass Fusing

Project 5 - Nightlight Shade

We love the combination of art glass and light, and one of the easiest ways to combine the two is to create a nightlight. They make great gifts since nearly everyone can find a handy place for one. A nightlight is easy to design, the simpler the better and I encourage you to customize your own pattern. However, you must keep these mini-shades small because a larger shade will sag under its own weight in the outlet socket mount.

The shade on the left was fired with the décor side up while the shade on the right was reverse fired, décor side down.

One noticeable difference on the reverse fired shade (right) is the design strips have more edge definition. What you can't see in the photo is how the surface of the reverse fired shade has taken on the subtle texture of the Thinfire™ paper.

(The difference in shape of these two lights is due to a different shape of the base glass and is not a result of the fuse firing.)

HotTip

It should go without saying but perhaps I do need to point out, that the colors and glass combinations that I used for the projects in this book reflect my personal style and taste. You can probably tell that I am partial to red, yellow, orange and blues contrasted against dark colors. I love these color combinations but I don't expect you to be as excited by them as I am. So let the creative ideas flow, experiment with whatever color combination turns you on, and most of all have fun!

What You'll Learn

- Reverse Firing (firing with the design side towards kiln shelf)
- Compare reverse firing with regular firing (decorations on top side)

Tools & Equipment

- Glass cutting tools
- Glass cleaning supplies
- Kiln, kiln controller and shelf

Materials

- E-6000™ Adhesive
- Night light fixture with clip (plastic or metal)
- Thinfire™ paper or prepared Kiln shelf
- Glass (either COE but all glass must be the same):
  - 3" x 7" (8 x 18 cm) dark green, cath iridescent
  - 3" x 7" (8 x 18 cm) red, cathedral

Step-by-Step Instructions

For this project we want to create 2 items that are almost the same, except we are going to fire them a little differently. One will be fired with the 'décor on top' and the other will be done in a reverse firing with the 'décor down' against the shelf. Try this little experiment, I think the results will surprise you.

1. We need to cut 2 similar pieces for every glass component in this project. Start by tracing (or drawing freehand) the shape for the nightlight on the background glass color that you have chosen.

2. Next we will create the design elements. I decided to cut 3 curved strips from the dark green iridescent to use for my accent but you may want to create a totally different design using squares, triangles or any combination of shapes or colors that your heart desires. Just remember to cut 2 pieces of each component, one for each of the 2 nightlights we're making.

Introduction to Glass Fusing

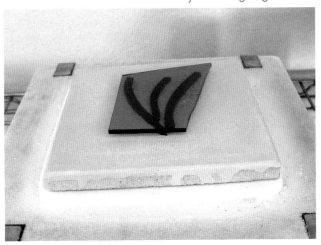

3. Now we will setup and assemble the components in preparation for the fuse firing. Clean and dry all glass components. Place one of the background base pieces on your prepared kiln shelf (either kiln washed or covered with Thinfire™ paper) smooth side up. Then arrange the décor pieces (curved stripes) on the base glass with the iridescent side up.

4. Place the shelf in your kiln and fire it according to the steps presented in The Kiln Firing Process on page 25. Use the firing chart on page 37 designed for Small/Med Components - Full Fuse - 2 Layers. If your kiln shelf is large enough to accommodate 2 night-lights you could do this second "reverse fired" night-light in the same firing. Just make sure to leave at least 1/2" (13 mm) between the 2 nightlights.

5. To setup this "reverse fired" nightlight lay the décor strips iridescent side down on the shelf then place the background base on top of the décor strips. It doesn't really matter if the base piece is smooth side down or not. If you're fusing with an opal glass you may want the side with the most interesting pattern placed down because this will be the outward facing side in the finished nightlight. See photos at the top of this page for details on this reverse fire set up.

6. Place the assembly into the kiln and fire using the same firing schedule you used for the first nightlight - on page 37.

7. Finish the night-lights by gluing the plastic (or metal) clip-holders to the back of the glass lampshade. We've experimented with many different adhesives, and found that E-6000™ works best for us, especially when gluing glass to plastic or metal.

> **Hot Tip**
>
> When gluing glass to any other material (including another piece of glass) it is imperative to thoroughly clean all areas where the adhesive will go with rubbing alcohol before applying the glue. And here's a ProTip, experienced fusers refer to gluing as "cold fusing" just because it just sounds more refined.

Now let's compare the results of these two different methods of firing. Notice that the face side of the reverse fired nightlight is flat and the décor design appears to be pushed into the base glass and the edge lines are more defined. In addition, the face surface has taken on the texture of the shelf or Thinfire™ paper and it's not as shinny as the standard face-up fired nightlight. This technique can be used to great effect when designing items where you want crisp lines between contrasting colors or where a matt finish surface texture is suitable.

Project 6 – Circle Nugget Making

I made a pair of simple little earrings that I love to wear and my students often ask me how I manage to cut such "perfect little circles" for them. I tell them that I didn't have to cut circles; instead I cut squares and let the kiln form the circles for me. So before you attempt to score, break and grind your glass into precise little disks let me introduce you to a simple process that has many different applications for creating components for fused pieces.

Step-by-Step Instructions

1. We will need about 10 pieces of glass that are 1/4" (6.5 mm) square, another 10 that are 1/2" (13 mm) square, and another 10 that are 3/4" (20 mm) square. The easiest way to create a bunch of little square glass pieces, is to cut a long narrow strip and then score and break it into smaller square pieces. So we'll need to score and break one strip from the colored glass and one strip from the clear glass of each size in the materials list.

ProTip: I like to use my Morton Portable Workshop 'cutting bar and stop' for this. Using this jig system for scoring I can quickly create dozens of squares that are exact copies. Also the Morton 'button and bar' breaker method is a great way to break out these long narrow strips. The Morton Workshop comes with detailed instructions to explain these techniques.

2. To create narrow strips by hand use a ruler to measure and mark the first strip size on your glass (start with the 3/4" - 20 mm strip, it's easier). Score the glass and position it flat on your bench with the score parallel to the edge. Now use your glass pliers to grasp the strip close to one end of the score. Hold the glass securely on the bench with one hand and pull on the pliers (as if you were trying to tear the glass like you would a piece of cloth) then snap down. The break should follow along the score and you should have a 3/4" (20 mm) x 6" (15 cm) narrow strip. Repeat this step for the other strip sizes and for the strips from the clear glass as well.

3. Dividing the strips into squares is much easier than cutting the long narrow strips. Simply measure and mark off the squares on each strip, then score and break them out.

What You'll Learn

- How to create small flat spheres - a.k.a. nuggets
- How to score and break narrow strips of glass

Tools & Equipment

- Glass cutting tools
- Glass cleaning supplies
- Kiln, kiln controller and shelf
- Morton Portable Workshop (optional)

Materials

- Glass (all glass must be the same COE):
  - 6" x 6" (15 x 15 cm) piece of colored cathedral
  - 6" x 6" (15 x 15 cm) piece of clear cathedral
- 5 1/4" x 5 1/4" (14 x 14 cm) Thinfire™ paper

Introduction to Glass Fusing

This pre-fire setup photograph has several nuggets ready to fire. The numbers indicate how many glass layers each stack contains. Study the after-firing photograph below to compare how the quantity and make-up of glass layers influences the shape and size and color of the finished nugget.

This is the same shelf setup after it was taken to a full fuse firing. Comparing the shapes and colors of these nuggets will tell you a lot about how various thickness or color combinations react to full fuse temperatures.

4. To demonstrate the effect of single and multiple layers I've created this special firing with different layer heights. The numbers on the setup photograph indicates how many glass layers each stack contains.

5. Before you set up your first 'nugget' firing let's compare the pre-firing photograph at left, with the after-firing photograph, below left. Notice that the single layer 1/4" (6.5 mm) and 1/2" (13 mm) squares rounded off nicely, while the single layer 3/4" square (bottom right) is not totally round. Also observe how we stacked the bigger pieces to form a star pattern (bottom left) that also helps to create a more rounded nugget. Finally notice that the lighter blue circles were stacked with blue and clear glass together, while the darker circles used blue glass only.

6. Put the squares into a pan of warm water and dish detergent to soak, then remove and dry each one separately. Now arrange the pieces on a prepared kiln shelf (either primed using kiln wash or cut a piece of Thinfire™ paper to cover your kiln shelf) and place as many nuggets on the shelf as you can fit. Make small, medium and large ones and you could even make some with a top layer of decorative glass like Dichroic, iridescent, opalescent, whatever your heart desires. Just make sure the glass pieces you combine have the same COE. Place the nugget filled shelf on the kiln floor and fire up the kiln.

7. Fire according to the firing chart presented here for Jewelry Components - Full Fuse - 2+ Layers. When the kiln has reached 1500°F (816°C) open the lid and take a peek (be sure to wear your safety glasses - it's hot in there!). The glass should be fully fused with a nice rounded top, comparable to the nuggets you see in this after-firing picture. If they are not quite there, close the lid and check again in a few minutes when the kiln has reached 1700°F (927°C). When you are satisfied with the results, turn off your kiln, vent it by raising the lid until the kiln has cooled to around 1100°F (590°C). Then close the lid and let it cool to room temperature at its own pace (this could be anywhere from 4 to 6 hours).

JEWELRY COMPONENTS - FULL FUSE - 2+ LAYERS				
Phase	*Temp/Min*	*Arrive Temp*	*SoakTime*	*Action*
Temp Up	30°F / 18°C	1000°F / 538°C	1 min	Remove Vent
Temp Up	Full-speed	*1500°F / 816°C	10+/- min	Observe
Flash Cool	High-speed	1100°F / 593°C	0 min	Open & Close Lid
Temp Hold	5°F / 3°C	955°F / 513°C	10 min	Hold your fire
Cool Down	Undisturbed	100°F / 38°C	N/A	Do Not Peek

* 'Arrive' Temperature will vary; it is essential to 'Observe' your project carefully as it approaches.

Introduction to Glass Fusing

HotTip

Stay with your kiln the entire time to ensure you don't miss those critical full fuse temperatures. This entire firing - from cold kiln to fused - should not take more than 30 to 40 minutes. I cannot begin to tell you how many times I've been side tracked and the next thing you know I have to deal with an over fired kiln load - this is not a pretty sight.

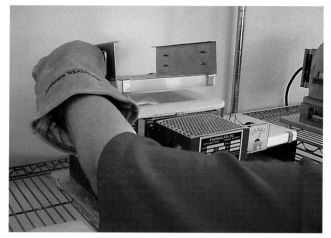

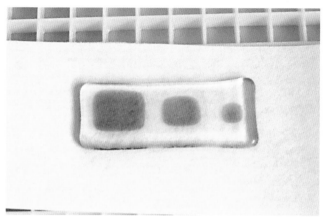

8. Comparing the two photos above you'll see what happens when a single layer square is fused directly into a background glass. Notice that these squares stay more or less square. However if one of the pre-fired circle nuggets were fired into the a similar background glass, it would produce a perfect circle.

9. So now we have nuggets. What do we do with them? As I mentioned earlier, I've used them to create simple earrings by gluing a matching pair onto earring posts. They can be incorporated into other fuse firings as decorative touches, especially when you need a dot or a nice round circle (for eyes or buttons for example).

10. I use these nuggets constantly in my work and I try to keep a good stock on hand at all times. Whenever I am doing a full-fuse firing I take the opportunity to fill any empty spaces on the kiln shelf with nuggets (remember to leave enough space in between the fuse pieces). I keep my 'extra stock' nuggets in plastic tubs separated and clearly marked as COE 90 and COE System 96 nuggets.

HotTip

You can make some really stunning nuggets by using a special piece of glass for the top layer. Sometimes I have tiny shards of dichroic glass left over from a different project and I love to place one or two pieces on the top layer of a nugget, the result is stunning!

We call these items nuggets but as soon as you fancy them up with bits of Dichroic glass (see next project) or other decorative glass, a nugget suddenly becomes a 'cabochon'. A cabochon is a term borrowed from the jewelry industry and is defined as 'a gem or bead in convex form and highly polished but not faceted. Doesn't that sound like the item we've just made? The only difference between these two is panache and a better press agent.

Introduction to Glass Fusing

Project 7 – Jewelry Pendants

When I started to write this book I wasn't sure if I should include a chapter on jewelry. I know there are already some excellent books out there (see ProTip on page 45). After some discussion with my publisher we came to the conclusion that a book titled 'Introduction to Glass Fusing' would not be complete without some basics on fused glass jewelry making.

What You'll Learn

- Make a slide pendant without drilling a hole
- Dichroic glass -art glass 'all dressed up'

Tools & Equipment

- Glass cutting tools
- Scissors (for cutting fiber paper)
- Tweezers
- White glue
- Glass cleaning supplies
- Kiln, kiln controller and shelf

Materials

- Fiber Paper 1/8" thick - small piece
- Glass (either COE but all glass must be the same):
  - Assorted colors of cathedral and/or opal glass
  - Dichroic glass for special design accents

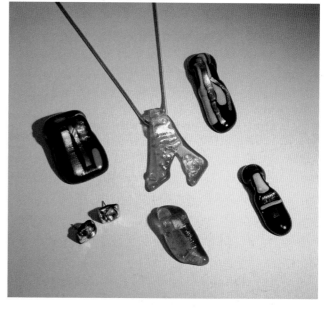

Step-By-Step Instructions

1. When I am in the mood to make some pendants I like to pick out an assortment of glass and spread it out so I can see what I have. The first thing we have to do, is choose a base color and cut two pieces of glass that are approximately the same size and shape. These will be the bottom and top of the pendant. You can make your pendant any size you want. Our pendants normally range anywhere from 3/8" to 1-1/2" (1.0 to 3.8 cm) wide by 1" to 2 1/2" (2.5 to 6.5 cm) long. It's important to remember the larger the pendant the more it will weigh and since it will be hanging from someone's neck (maybe your own) you don't want it to be too heavy.

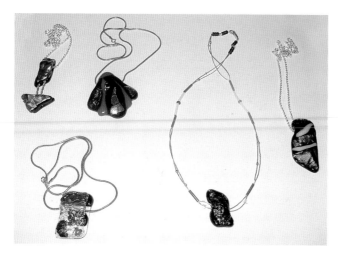

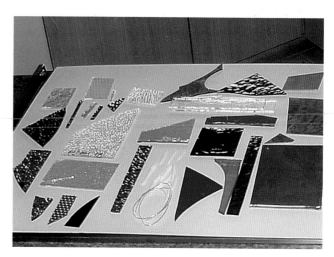

2. I am setting up to make 4 different pendants. We need 2 pieces cut for the main pendant base and 2 small pieces from the same glass approximately 3/16" (5 mm) square (or perhaps a rectangle, depends on the size and shape of your pendant). These pieces will be used to support and level the top glass.

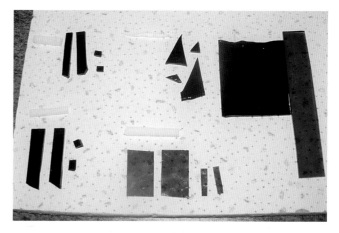

3. Use scissors to cut a strip of fiber paper that is 1/4" (6.5 mm) wide. Now cut this strip into pieces that are 1/2" (13 mm) longer than the width of each glass pendant (cut one piece for each pendant). These fiber paper pieces will form the slip hole in the pendant that will allow a neck chain to pass through.

ProTip: If you have a particular neck chain that you intend to use with this pendant, make sure to cut the fiber paper strip so it is slightly fatter than the clasp on the end of the chain.

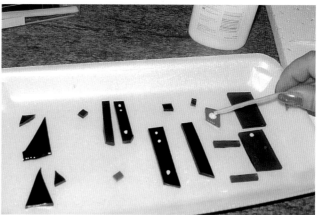

4. Clean the glass pieces with rubbing alcohol (or dish detergent and warm water) and place them on a clean tray (I like to recycle those foam food trays from the supermarket for this). Choose one base piece from each pendant set. Place a tiny dot of white glue on the base glass at the very top, then position one of the 3/16" (5 mm) square pieces on the glue to line up with the top edge (do this for each pendant). Now put a drop of white glue directly below this first glass square and lay the fiber paper strip across the base glass. Finally position the second small square piece in the last third of your base. Place a tiny dot of white glue on the 2 small squares and cover everything with the top piece. Do not move them until the glue is completely dry.

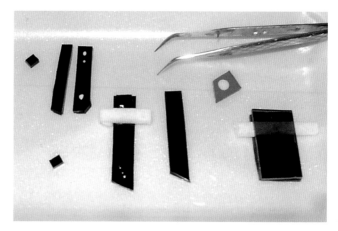

ProTip: We use white glue for our fabrication but there are glues made specifically for fusing. The glue will hold your pieces together as you continue to build on it with decoration pieces and when moving it to the kiln. This fabrication glue will burn off during firing but it's best to use as little as possible. Too much glue can discolor and stain or it may cause unwanted air bubbles to form.

5. Next we'll choose and cut the décor pieces (while waiting for the glue to dry). Dichroic glass décor pieces will give these pendants a dramatic effect. However, I have seen beautiful pendants made from combinations of standard fusing colors (remember COE's don't mix). You will notice that I have used a combination of Dichroic and regular glass for my pendant design. Clean these décor pieces, put a dab of glue on them and position them on the pendant.

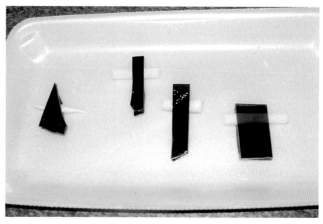

6. When you have finished the assembly, place your pendants on a prepared kiln shelf (either primed or with Thinfire™ paper). Place the kiln shelf (with your glass) in the kiln and fire it according to the schedule on page 41 for Jewelry Components - Full Fuse - 2+ Layers.

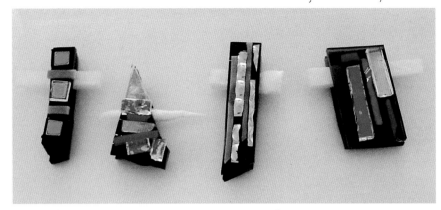

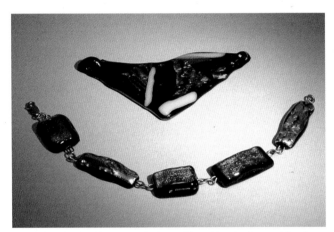

This bracelet has loops made from 'fine silver' wire and fired between the layers of glass then it was chained together using silver jump rings.

ProTip: There are many ways to create beautiful jewelry pieces using this basic fusing method. Hopefully the photo here as well as the 2 on page 43 will inspire you to use your imagination, combined with the various techniques from this book, to come up with your own unique creations. For instance you could drill a 5/64" (2 mm) hole using the high-speed hand drill and use wire wrapping techniques to create the hanging loop. You could 'cold fuse' (glue) traditional jewelry findings to create pendants, earrings, brooch pins, bolo ties, and bracelets to name only a few ideas for jewelry. If you enjoy glass jewelry making you should look for Jayne Persico's book on fused glass and wire jewelry titled *'Innovative Adornments'*, with dozens of glass jewelry projects.

Dichroic Coatings - Enchanted Glass

Bedazzled is the only way I can describe how a person feels the first time they catch sight of a piece of dichroic art glass. It really does have a sort of magical enchantment that takes your breath away for just a moment. Currently, there is only a handfull of companies who have the very specialized equipment needed to coat glass with this amazing metallic surface. One of these companies is Coatings by Sandberg and when I met Mr. Sandberg at a show he tried to explain the manufacturing process to me, let me assure you that it sounded every bit as sophisticated as the glass itself appears. Actually it's not really important to know how it's made but you do need some basic information on how to use it.

Dichroic coating companies start with the same tested compatible glass that we use for fusing. This means you must use the same COE dichroic as the other glass in each fuse firing. As a rule coating companies use only black or clear glass for dichroic coating purposes. It is easy to see the dichroic colors reflecting off the surface of the black-coated glass (a.k.a. dichro/black); while with the surface of the clear-coated glass (a.k.a. dichro/clear) has a more subtle effect. Several effects are possible depending on how you use these in combination with other glass. Dichro/clear fired on a base of colored glass with the coated side up will produce a 'metallic look' surface. Dichro/clear fired with the coated side down will create a 'perception of depth' because you're looking through the clear layer to the dichroic coating below. You can get a similar effect with dichro/black by firing it coated side up and placing a clear layer on top.

Some artists combine multiple layers of dichroic to achieve an extraordinary display but you should not place coated side to coated side, as this combination does not usually fuse together successfully. This is also true when using dichroic and iridescent glass in the same project. Other than that, don't be afraid to experiment with your own combinations of art glass and dichroic coated glass, you may discover a spectacular merger.

Project 8 - Round Mini-Trays (A set of Two)

It's no secret among my students that I love to use triangles in much of my artwork, but I have to admit that every once in a while, when a student gets the idea to do something round, I appreciate the circle as a useful design feature. So this lesson is for those of you (dare I say, most of you) who are looking for more from your art than simply triangles.

The inspiration for these cute little plates came from a pair of beautiful trays that my friend Suyako brought me from her last trip to Japan. I think they have a wonderful shape I just love the way the little squared-off indent interferes with the otherwise perfect symmetry of the circle.

What You'll Learn

- Circle Cutting, scoring both freehand and using a circle cutter
- Making and firing with a fiber paper mold

Tools & Equipment

- Permanent marker
- A drawing compass
- Glass cutting tools
- A circle glass cutter (optional)
- Glass grinder (optional)
- X-acto™ knife and Scissors
- Glass cleaning supplies
- Kiln, kiln controller and shelf

Materials

- Glass (either COE but all glass must be the same):
  - 7" x 12" (17.8 x 30.5 cm) red, cath iridescent
  - 4" x 1" (10.2 x 2.5 cm) black, opalescent
  - 4" x 1" (10.2 x 2.5 cm) white, opalescent
- Fiber paper - 1/8" x 6" x 12" (4mm x 15 x 30 cm)
- Thinfire™ paper (or prepared kiln shelf)

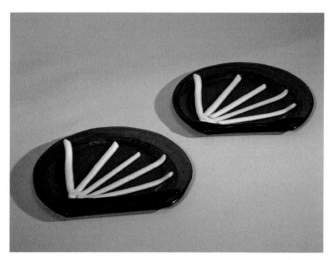

My friend Suyako gave me this pair of beautiful trays as a gift from her recent trip to Japan. I love the simplicity of the design and of course the play of the red against the black background.

Step-by-Step Instructions

1. For some reason people new to glass cutting are often intimidated at the prospect of cutting and breaking a circle. The fact is, circle cutting is really quite simple and forgiving since the tendency is for the glass to break away from the center and that is what you want anyway. Any points left on the edge can be removed with grozing pliers and smoothed with a grinder. First we'll create our pattern using the compass to layout a 5" (12.7 cm) diameter circle on a piece of heavy stock paper. You could also cut the flat edge on the pattern at this point but we will leave ours a complete circle for this disk cutting demonstration.

2. Position the 5" (12.7 cm) disk pattern on your background glass about a 1/4" to 1/2" (6 to 13 mm) in from the glass edge and trace it with a marker (we used a white 'paint-pen' marker for ours). You could place the pattern in a corner on a larger sheet but it is easier to break out the circle if you cut a strip from the larger sheet wide enough for the disk.

3. Glass has a tendency to break in a straight line rather than follow the circle and we will make some relief scores to accommodate for this. We have drawn these relief lines on our glass for this demonstration but it is not necessary for you to do this every time.

4. Now we'll use our trusty glasscutter to make a score completely around the perimeter of the circle. This is one of the few times you will make a score that does not start at an edge and end at another edge. Start anywhere and make a score about 1/4 way around, stop and turn the glass then make sure you get the cutter wheel back into the score and continue around until you've come back to the starting point. The next step is to break out the score but let's take a look at some special tools to use as an alternate method for circle scoring.

5. The 'stop, turn and restart' scoring process is awkward and as you might expect there are special tools that make disk scoring easier. The model shown here is fully adjustable for circles from 3" to 24" (8 to 60 cm) diameter but there are many models to choose from so you will want to ask your supplier about the ones they carry. As a bonus many of these cutter jigs have a dual purpose and can be used for strip cutting as well.

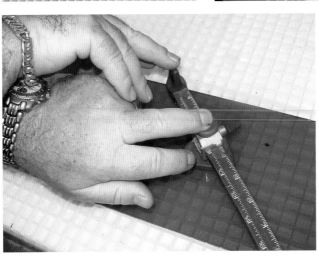

6. Use the built-in ruler on the jig to 'dial-in' the circle size, dip the wheel in cutter lubricant (most of these cutters do not have automatic oil feed), position the jig pivot point on the glass and do a 'dry run' to make sure the score will be in the right place. Finally put some pressure on the cutter head and slowly turn it to make the score all the way around the disk perimeter. Be careful to stop when you've reached the starting point, don't go over a score twice - it will not help the score and may damage the cutting wheel!

7. Now we'll break out the score. It doesn't matter if you made the score by hand or with a circle jig, the breaking process is the same. If you have a Morton workshop this is one of those times it is indispensable, the 'button and bar' breaker is perfect for breaking out circles. Position the score over the button and use the bar to just start the break, Now move the glass over the button a little further around the circle and use the bar to continue the break. Continue to move the glass, apply pressure with the bar, move the glass, etc. until you have returned to the starting point. You should be able to see the crack completely around the circle (look at it from the back) if some areas are not cracked yet put those spots over the button and apply pressure with the bar.

8. If you don't have a Morton 'button and bar' breaker you can break the glass by hand as well. Try tapping under the score with the butt end of your cutter to start the break, move along the score until you have a crack all the way around the disk.

9. We will score a few relief lines to allow the circle to break out easily. Some crafters make their relief score from a glass edge directly to the circle score (to meet at 90°). Our method is to make a few scores at more of a tangent. These come from an edge to meet the score at an angle. Truth is it makes very little difference where or how you make the relief scores, as long as you've cracked the circle all the way around before you make them.

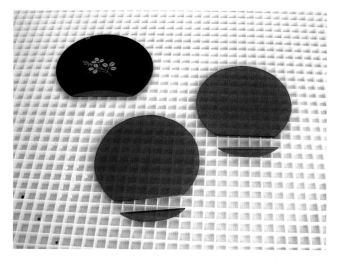

10. Now start by breaking the circle away from the main glass by hand, then use your grozer/breaker pliers to 'pull and snap' the rest of the edge pieces. You should end up with a fairly smooth circle with very few flares or points.

11. Now score and break the second disk. You may want to use a glass grinder (if you have one) to touch up any stray points that may be left on the disks' edge.

12. Since you now have 2 perfect circles you might choose to make round trays, but we want to follow the design concept inspired by the trays from Japan and that means we need to score and break the squared-off edge piece on both circles.

Introduction to Glass Fusing

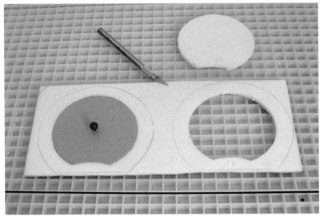

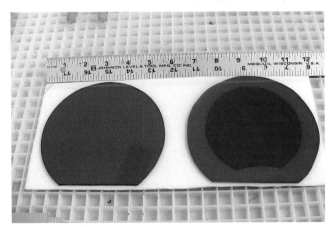

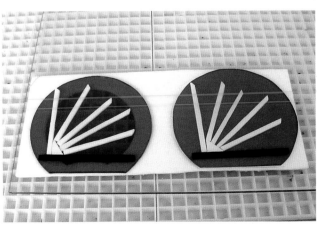

13. Now we'll make the fiber paper mold. We will be using our larger kiln for these trays so we will cut two molds from the same piece of fiber paper. If you're working with a smaller kiln cut only one mold. Measure and cut a piece of fiber paper slightly larger than the tray(s) and trace the outside perimeter of each tray blank on to the fiber paper.

14. Next use a compass to draw a circle on cardboard that is 1" (2.5 cm) smaller than the diameter of your glass blanks. This will allow 1/2" (1.3 cm) border for the dropout. If you are creating the squared-off circle as we are, you will also need to cut a flat side on your cardboard pattern 1/2" smaller than the glass blank.

15. Place your cardboard pattern on the fiber paper positioned in the center of the circle you traced from your glass blank and trace the pattern. We like to put a sheet of clear glass under the fiber paper to provide a flat stable base for our knife blade.

16. Use an X-acto™ knife to cut the fiber paper following along the cardboard pattern outline. Remove the fiber paper disc from the center. If you're making 2 at one time trace and cut the second mold as well.

17. We're ready to create our décor accent pieces and assemble the glass for firing. We used 5 thin strips of white opal just to keep it simple. You may want to create a geometric design or perhaps a stylized flower similar to the design on the original Japanese trays. Finish by cleaning the glass and drying each piece thoroughly then arrange the décor pieces on the discs - use a little assembly glue if necessary.

This plate was flat fused and then formed in a fiber paper slumping mold similar to the mold for the trays in this project.

Introduction to Glass Fusing

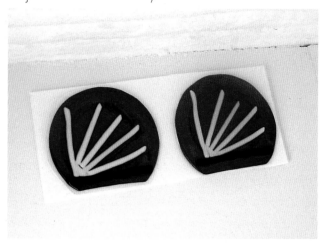

18. Place the fiber paper mold on the kiln shelf. Then lay a piece of Thinfire™ paper over the dropout mold and finally place your assembled glass on the mold being very careful to center it, this is especially important if you are creating the squared-off circle.

19. Fire the glass according to the chart present here for Medium Components - Full Fuse - 2 Layers.

20. After the kiln has cooled to room temperature remove your finished tray and take a moment to enjoy and examine the result. If you notice anything unusual try to determine what may have caused it and how to avoid it in the future however it may be an unexpected positive result or a "happy accident" that you may want to know how to repeat.

HotTip

Normally fiber paper can be used for only one firing as it tends to soften and break apart. But you can get another firing out of it if you simply leave it on the shelf and dust the mold and shelf with dry kiln wash powder. We use a nylon stocking filled with kiln wash powder for this (see page 35). If you are using fiberboard kiln shelves (we use Kaiser Lee™ Board), you can simply place the fiber paper mold directly on the fiberboard shelf, dust everything with kiln wash powder then place your assembled glass on the mold. You should do this for both the first and second firing as an easy and reliable way to prevent your glass from sticking.

MEDIUM COMPONENTS - FULL FUSE - 2 LAYERS

Phase	Temp/Min	Arrive Temp	SoakTime	Action
Temp Up	15°F / 9°C	1000°F / 538°C	1 min	Remove Vent
Temp Up	Full-speed	*1450°F / 788°C	10+/- min	Observe
Flash Cool	High-speed	1100°F / 593°C	0 min	Open & Close Lid
Temp Hold	5°F / 3°C	955°F / 513°C	15 min	Hold your fire
Cool Down	Undisturbed	100°F / 38°C	N/A	Do Not Peek

* 'Arrive' Temperature will vary; it is essential to 'Observe' your project carefully as it approaches.

HotTip

Annealing requires a controlled cooling of the glass through a specific temperature range and it is a critical step to ensuring the fused object will be free from internal stress. Glass that is not properly annealed could break spontaneously in the kiln during cool down or at any time subsequent to its' removal from the kiln - even a year or more after firing!

Each category of glass has a specific ideal annealing temperature. However annealing will take place as long as the glass is held within 20 to 30°F (14 to 16°C) of its' ideal annealing temperature, the farther away from the specific 'ideal' temperature the more soaking time it will take. All tested compatible glass that we use in this book has an ideal annealing temperature range between 970°F & 940°F (520°C & 505°C). Annealing time increases with size and thickness of the glass. Pieces with bigger mass need more time to cool down to room temperature and that is why we have specified a cool down phase in the our charts to allow for this requirement.

Project 9 - Decorative Serving Trays

Now that we have a few projects under our belt I thought it would be fun to create 3 different trays, using a single piece of fiber paper to make the molds. You will need a mid-sized kiln with a minimum 13" (33 cm) firing chamber to make the larger tray (of course you could make that tray a little smaller). The other 2 smaller trays can easily be made in one of the small kilns.

Decorative flat trays are useful for many things. Of course we love them for serving sushi but they are also wonderful for serving snacks, deserts, and other foods. Don't overlook their value in the office, bedroom or bathroom to organize desks and dressers.

What You'll Learn

- Making molds with 1/8" (4 mm) Fiber Paper
- Fuse firing larger sized glass with 2 layers
- Firing iridescent side down

Tools & Equipment

- Permanent marker
- Glass cutting tools
- Glass grinder (optional)
- X-acto™ knife and Scissors (for fiber paper)
- Small strainer or Nylon stocking, for shelf primer
- Glass cleaning supplies
- Kiln, kiln controller and shelf

Materials

- Glass (either COE but all glass must be the same):
  - 8" x 12" (20.3 x 30.5 cm) clear
  - 12" x 12" (30.5 x 30.5 cm) red, cath iridescent
  - 12" x 12" (30.5 x 30.5 cm) blue, cath, iridescent
  - 2" x 12" (5.1 x 30.5 cm) green, cath, iridescent
- Fiber Paper
  - 1/8" (4 mm) thick - 8" x 12" (20.3 x 30.5) sheet, for mold making
  - 1/8" (4 mm) thick - Size to cover kiln shelf, needed as insulation between clay shelf and glass
- Powdered shelf primer in a nylon stocking to sprinkle on mold and shelf

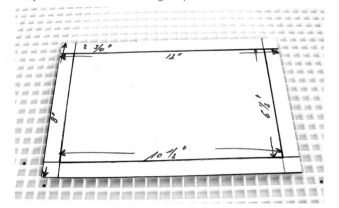

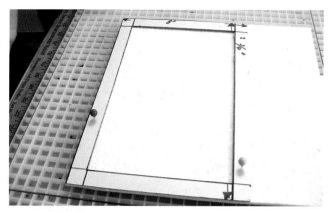

Step-by-Step Instructions

1. The first step is to create the mold forms. We will cut them all from one piece of 1/8" (4 mm) thick - 8" x 12" (20.3 x 30.5 cm) fiber paper. We prefer to cut a pattern for the molds using a piece of cardboard the same size as the fiber paper. Then, lay the cardboard pattern on the fiber paper and follow along the pattern edge using an X-acto™ knife to cut the fiber paper. Measure and draw the 8" x 12" (20.3 x 30.5 cm) on your pattern. Now make a 3/4" (1.9 cm) inside border all around and cut the cardboard pattern.

2. Use the center cut-out piece and layout a 5" x 5" (12.7 x 12.7 cm) square with a 3/4" (1.9 cm) border all around. Now draw a wavy line diagonally across the center to create a divider that is 1/4" (6.4 mm) wide. Cut out this pattern using an X-acto™ knife.

3. Next we'll cut the fiber paper molds. Pin the large pattern on the fiber paper and follow along the edge using an X-acto™ knife to cut and remove the center section. Your first slump mold is ready.

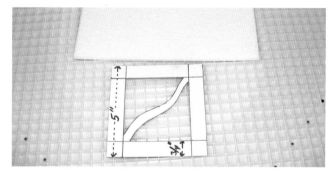

4. Now, we'll create a 2nd mold, using the fiber paper removed from the center. Cut two 5" (12.7 cm) squares from the left over paper using the 5" square cardboard pattern as your guide. We are going to stack these 2 molds to make a single mold that will be 1/4" (7.5 cm) deep. This will allow us to make a 5" square tray with two compartments that will be twice as deep as the larger tray.

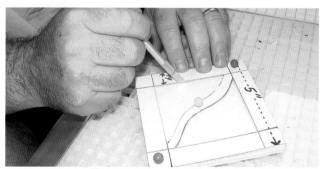

5. The four triangle pieces cut from the center will also be stacked two high and used as drape molds. This photo shows how all three mold will look when finished. Remember, the 5" x 5" (12.7 x 12.7 cm) square mold and the smaller triangle molds are stacked two layers high.

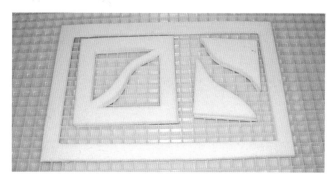

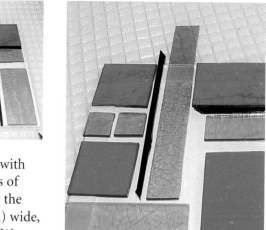

6. As always, our design is just a suggestion. Feel free to come up with your own personal creation. Just remember to stay with 2 full layers of glass. The bottom layer is clear glass, the same size of the mold. For the décor we used several strips. The dark green strips are 1/4"(6.4 mm) wide, while the blue and red strips are either 1" or 2" (2.5 or 5 cm) wide. We played around with our design and finally settled on this arrangement.

7. The next tray we'll make is the 5" (12.7 cm) square that will have 2 slumped compartments. The base glass is of course 5" (12.7 cm) square, we used a blue cathedral, then we added some red corners and a dark blue center design.

8. Lastly we will cut the shapes and design for the twin trays. We started with another 5" (12.7 cm) square glass, this time we used a piece of iridized red cathedral. Since these trays are going to be draped over the mold we will place the iridized side down.

ProTip: The iridized coating is less likely to stick to the mold, plus it will become the topside when the trays are finished.

Photo above: The 2 compartment square tray is cut and placed on the slump mold and ready to go into the kiln.

Photo at left: The fused and draped twin triangle trays. These have a simple design with an iridized inside surface.

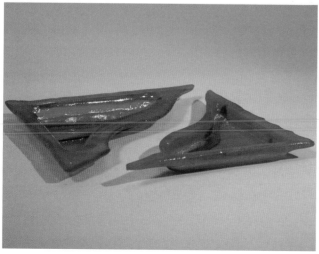

Introduction to Glass Fusing

9. Clean and dry all the glass pieces very thoroughly. Assemble both the larger rectangular tray and the 5" (12.7 cm) square tray in the following order on your kiln shelf:

- 1/8" (3.2 mm) fiber paper to cover the kiln shelf, this will act as an insulation between the glass and the clay mold. If you're using fiberboard as a kiln shelf the fiber paper is not necessary because the fiber-board does not retain heat

- The fiber paper molds you just created. The 5" (12.7 cm) mold is a double stacked fiber layer

- Kiln wash dust - sprinkle it on to cover the mold and the kiln shelf, use a small kitchen strainer or use a nylon stocking filled with kiln wash

- Your assembled glass tray with décor glass in place

10. The triangular trays are a drape and are placed in the kiln in a different order:

- 1/8" (3.2 mm) fiber paper to insulate the clay kiln shelf

- Two fiber paper molds, these are also double stacked layers

- Kiln wash dust - sprinkle to cover the mold and kiln shelf

- Place blue glass strips, iridescent side down on fiber paper molds

- Place the red glass triangles iridescent side down on top of each mold and make sure the fiber paper mold is in the center of your red glass

11. Finally, place the kiln shelf with all the molds into the kiln and fire using the schedule at right for Medium/Large Components - Full Fuse - 2 Layers.

HotTip

Fiber paper molds are easy to make and versatile to use and we use them often. However, if you use a clay kiln shelf you must cover it with a piece of fiber paper to act as an insulation buffer between your glass and shelf. Fiber Paper is an insulation material that does not conduct heat like a clay shelf. Without an insulation buffer the resulting uneven heat distribution could cause stress fractures. If you use a fiberboard (i.e. Kaiser Lee Board) as a kiln shelf, you only need Primo™ primer kiln wash or Thinfire™ paper as a release. Fiberboard is an insulation material like fiber paper and causes no stress due to uneven heating and cooling.

This is a photo of my large kiln fully loaded prior to a fuse firing. At top left is the Large Tray project, at lower left is the small tray with 2 compartments and lower right is the Twin Triangle Trays. Since I had the space, I took the opportunity to create a whole bunch of cabochons (upper right). I hate to fire a kiln that is partly empty.

MED/LARGE COMPONENTS - FULL FUSE - 2 LAYERS				
Phase	*Temp/Min*	*Arrive Temp*	*SoakTime*	*Action*
Temp Up	12°F / 7°C	1000°F / 538°C	1 min	Remove Vent
Temp Up	Full-speed	*1450°F / 788°C	10+/- min	Observe
Flash Cool	High-speed	1100°F / 593°C	0 min	Open & Close Lid
Temp Hold	5°F / 3°C	955°F / 513°C	30 min	Hold your fire
Temp Down	3°F / 2°C	750°F / 400°C	1 min	Do Not Peek
Cool Down	Undisturbed	100°F / 38°C	N/A	Do Not Peek

* 'Arrive' Temperature will vary; it is essential to 'Observe' your project carefully as it approaches.

Introduction to Glass Fusing

Project 10 – Frit-Cast Dolphin

Frit casting means you place small pieces of glass - called frit, into a dam mold (I'm not swearing at the mold, dam is the type of mold) and fuse it together. This is one way to achieve irregular shapes. Others would be cutting the dolphin shape with a glass saw or piecing it together with individual cut glass pieces, similar to fabricating stained glass.

Making a dolphin or any other shape in this way is a lot of fun. You can play the colors while using up a lot of your scrap glass. Frit is also available commercially, packaged in different sizes and colors and makes frit casting even easier by eliminating the frit making step.

What You'll Learn

- Making a Dam Mold using Fiber Paper
- Cutting Frit with a Mosaic Cutter
- Making and Placing a Wire Hook
- Fire Polish & Round-Off an Edge

Tools & Equipment

- Glass cutting tools
- Mosaic Cutter (optional)
- X-acto™ knife & Scissors (for fiber)
- Glass cleaning supplies
- Kiln, kiln controller and shelf
- Glass grinder with standard and mini bit or Abrasive stone (instead of Grinder)

Needle Nosed Pliers

- Pair of Large Bent-nosed Tweezers

Materials

- Glass (either COE but all glass must be the same):

  - All cathedrals in clear, orange, green, & red, small irregular shaped scrap glass is fine

- Fiber paper - 1/8" x 6" x 8" (4 mm x 15 x 20.3 cm)
- Nichrome or Copper wire, 18-20 gauge
- Thinfire™ paper - 6" x 8" (15 x 20.3 cm)

Step-By-Step Instructions

1. Cut a pattern from a copy of the Dolphin drawing on page 56. I made my pattern using blue construction paper. Place the fiber paper on the clear sheet glass working surface and copy the outline of the dolphin to the paper with a pencil.

2. Cut the dolphin shape using an X-acto™ knife. Be sure to keep the fiber paper cutout dolphin for a future project. You could use it as a drape mold that will produce a shallow dish with a subtle relief design.

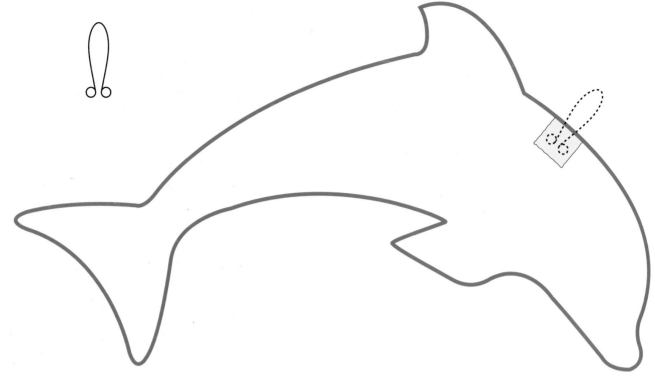

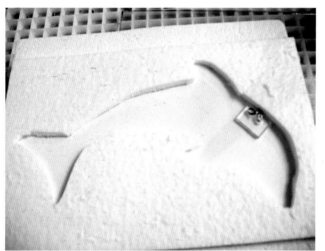

3. We need to form the hanging loop from a 2" (5 cm) long piece of nichrome or copper wire. Use needle nose pliers to shape it as shown in the full-size drawing (above left on this page).

4. Now we need to assemble the dam mold in the following order.

- Kiln shelf - does not have to be prepared

- Thinfire™ paper - glue it to the kiln shelf with a few drops white bond glue

- Fiber paper dam mold - glue it to the Thinfire™ paper with some white glue

- The final step is place a larger sized piece of clear frit glass right at the balance point on the Dolphin's back (see the yellow area in the drawing), for hanging the finished piece. Now push the wire loop into the fiber paper leaving only the curly ends of the hook sticking out. Use a drop of glue to secure the wire loop to the glass and another to glue the glass to the paper.

5. Cut several 1/4" (6.4 mm) or narrower strips of glass. For this project we are using red, orange, yellow, green and clear cathedrals. The strips do not have to be precise and they do not have to be long since we are going to break them into small bits anyway.

6. Clean each glass strip and dry them thoroughly.

7. Now we're going to divide these strips into small pieces. I was introduced to this mosaic cutter by Shelby Wilkinson, a mosaic artist and one of my students. It sure makes quick work of creating the frit pieces. Simply place the 'wheel-jaws' of the mosaic cutter at the very edge of the glass (not in the center) and squeeze the handles. Snap! Just like that the piece breaks off.

8. I hold the glass strip in my left hand and push it into the jaws, squeeze the handle and let the little piece fall into my hand (see photo). This prevents the piece from flying around when it breaks, when I have 3 or 4 in my hand I drop them into an old terry towel spread across my work area. I work with one color at a time and keep the colors separated on paper plates.

HotTip

Of course there are other ways to create frit. You could cut the narrow strips into frit-sized pieces by scoring every 1/4″ (6.4 mm) or so with your glasscutter and then break them. The only drawback is you'll need to clean the glass pieces again due of the cutter oil. I know some crafters like to put the glass between several sheets of old newspaper and smash it with a hammer. This can be dangerous and it is not as easy or as thorough as it sounds but I am told it can be a real stress reliever to get those aggressions out! Finally you could leave the frit making to the professionals and buy it already sorted into colors, sizes, and COE. This frit is available from your friendly local glass supplier.

9. By now the glue has dried on the mold and we can go ahead and load it with our frit. Use bent nose tweezers to place the clean glass pieces in your mold. Create a variety of shades by mixing clear into the second or third layer to lighten the intensity or use all colored glass for darker shades.

10. This photo shows the mold filled to a height of 3 layers to make it approximately level with the top of the fiber paper. This is the optimum thickness because fewer layers could cause holes to open up during firing and thicker will change the firing schedule for this project.

FRIT CASTING - FULL FUSE - 2-3 LAYERS				
Phase	*Temp/Min*	*Arrive Temp*	*Soak Time*	*Action*
Temp Up	30°F / 18°C	1000°F / 538°C	1 min	Remove Vent
Temp Up	Full-speed	*1480°F / 805°C	10+/- min	Observe
Flash Cool	High-speed	1100°F / 593°C	0 min	Open & Close Lid
Temp Hold	5°F / 3°C	955°F / 513°C	45 min	Hold your fire
Temp Down	3°F / 2°C	750°F / 400°C	1 min	Do Not Peek
Cool Down	Undisturbed	100°F / 38°C	N/A	Do Not Peek

* 'Arrive' Temperature will vary; it is essential to 'Observe' your project carefully as it approaches.

11. Place the entire assembly into your kiln and fire it according to the firing chart presented here for Frit Casting.

12. This photo shows the dolphin after firing. Notice the fiber paper dam still surrounding it. The fiber paper becomes soft during firing and it is not practical to reuse it as a frit cast dam. You may be able to salvage some of the larger sections for further use on other projects.

13. The paper residue left on your piece and possibly on the kiln shelf must be removed. The safest way to do this, is to use a plastic bucket filled with water. Simply dunk the fired piece into the pail to dissolve the paper and the paper particles. The paper particles will collect at the bottom making safe disposal easier. See HotTip on page 31.

14. Be careful while you're washing this frit cast item, you will more than likely find some sharp points (called spikes) around the edge of your fired piece. This is a result of the frit casting method (spikes may also occur when a piece is over fired). The photo at left clearly shows a number of these spikes, some are more severe than others but all need to be removed.

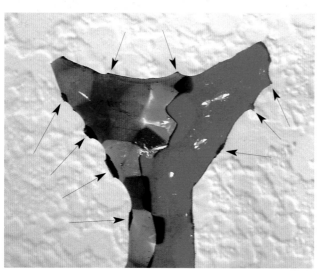

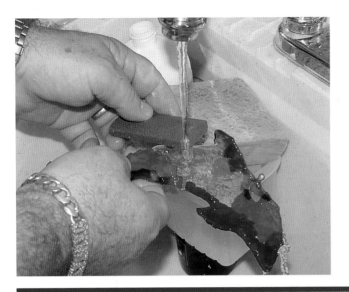

15. These spikes are hazardous but they come off easily by hand grinding using an abrasive stone or a diamond nail file. For best results always do this with the glass under water (either in a water bucket or under running water). You can use your glass grinder for this process but you must be careful that you do not over grind. Fire polishing will smooth and polish the edges but intense grinding and abrasion will often result in a murky haze like stain to appear on the edge after firing.

16. It is not absolutely necessary to fire polish after grinding but we think it gives the item a professional touch. This second firing will round off and polish the edge and it is simple to do.

MEDIUM COMPONENTS - FIRE POLISH - 1/4" (6MM) THICK				
Phase	*Temp/Min*	*Arrive Temp*	*SoakTime*	*Action*
Temp Up	5°F / 3°C	1000°F / 538°C	1 min	Remove Vent
Temp Up	Full-speed	*1350°F / 732°C	10+/- min	Observe
Flash Cool	High-speed	1100°F / 593°C	0 min	Open & Close Lid
Temp Hold	5°F / 3°C	955°F / 513°C	45 min	Hold your fire
Temp Down	3°F / 2°C	750°F / 400°C	1 min	Do Not Peek
Cool Down	Undisturbed	100°F / 38°C	N/A	Do Not Peek

* 'Arrive' Temperature will vary; it is essential to 'Observe' your project carefully as it approaches.

17. Clean and dry the dolphin thoroughly then place it on a prepared kiln shelf and fire according to the chart provided here at left.

ProTip: You will notice that this schedule has a much slower ramp up speed than any project presented in this book so far. The slower ramp speed is necessary to prevent thermal shock due to the current thickness of this dolphin.

This frit cast 'Spiderman' figure was created using the same fiber paper mold technique as we used for the Dolphin.

Then we added a twist during fire polishing by placing the flat-cast figure on a piece of fiber-board and allowing it to drape over until the legs flattened out on the kiln shelf. This turns our 1 dimensional 'Spiderman' into a 3-dimensional wall sculpture.

Introduction to Glass Fusing

Project 11 – Frit Cast Frog

You could cast this frog project in a fiber paper dam mold using the same technique we used to create the dolphin. The problem is, fiber paper is generally only a one time use mold. What if you had an item that you wanted to make several times? Perhaps you want to make 24 snowflakes to sell as Christmas tree ornaments, or you've decided to make 65 wedding bells to present to the honored guests.

What You'll Learn

• Carving fiberboard (Kaiser-Lee™ Board)

• 'Hole Punch' Pattern Transfer Technique

• Preparing board with Primo™ Primer

• Draping to create a 3-D sculpture

Tools & Equipment

• Glass cutting tools

• Mosaic Cutter (optional)

• X-acto™ knife (for fiber paper)

• Glass cleaning supplies

• Kiln, kiln controller and shelf

• Abrasive stone or Glass Grinder

• Pair of Large Bent-nosed Tweezers

• Punch needle, simply a knitting needle, a pushpin, a woodworker's awl, or even a sharp pencil.

• Dust Mask and Goggles

Materials

• Glass (either COE but all glass must be the same):

  - Glass used in the project example was: clear, apple green confetti and dark green iridescent

  - 2 pre-fused dichroic nuggets for the eyes

• Fiberboard (Kaiser-Lee™ Board) 1" x 8" x 9" (2.5 x 20 x 23 cm)

• Kiln & Kiln Shelf, medium/large firing chamber - 8" x 8" (20 x 20 cm) or larger

It would be time consuming and expensive to be forced to cut a new fiber paper mold for every item you want to make.

This is one of those instances where fiberboard is indispensable (naturally we're using Kaiser-Lee™ Board). Fiberboard can be used many times. In fact the mold for this frog has been used so many times that we have stopped counting.

The other major advantage is far fewer edge spikes are produced. This is mainly due to the fact that the fiberboard is coated with several layers of Primo™ Primer. We found out, quite by accident, that the more we used the frog mold the smoother the glass casting became and it was all because we apply a new coat of primer before each use. Now we do not even have to do a fire polishing when we use this mold.

Step-By-Step Instructions

1. Make a copy of the frog pattern on page 64 and secure it to the fiberboard using pushpins to prevent it from moving. Now transfer the outside perimeter lines from the pattern to the board by using a punch needle to poke holes through the paper pattern and into the fiberboard about 1/16" (2 mm) deep. You could also cut the pattern and trace with a pencil as we did in the dolphin project.

2. The punched holes are easier to see if they are colored. Dust the pattern using a nylon stocking filled with colored kiln wash (see page 10). Just pat the sock around the pattern and let the powder sift through the holes (use your dust mask while doing this). Remove the paper pattern from the board and put the excess kiln wash and the sock into a zip-lock plastic bag.

3. Next we need to carve the frog design into the fiberboard to a depth of about 3/8"(1 cm). Fiberboard is very soft and easy to carve. We used an old X-acto™ knife with a round tip blade (the blade doesn't have to be sharp). Over the years we have adapted a variety of simple tools for shaping and carving. For example, we have an old spoon & butter knife, several types of fingernail files, chopsticks, screwdrivers, putty knives and sometimes we use just our fingers to carve into the board - it really is that soft!

4. It will take some time to get the carving depth just right. You could carve more or less deep than the 3/8"(1 cm) but try to achieve a uniform depth. Also the bottom inside corners should be slightly rounded off, <u>do not</u> carve square or undercut corners.

5. When you have your mold carved the way you want it, you'll need to apply a few coats of shelf primer. Mix a batch of Primo Primer™ solution according to the product directions (we dilute one part primer powder with five parts water).

6. Apply the primer evenly to the finished mold using a hake brush. The board will quickly soak up the primer. So you will find that you'll need to re-load the brush often to cover only a small area with each stroke. Make sure the entire inside of the mold is fully covered with the primer. The photo on page 62 shows the entire inside and top surface coated with primer. It is not necessary to cover the top but sometimes we like to use this area to fuse other projects (like small cabochons) during the fuse firing.

Introduction to Glass Fusing

7. Now the hard part! You must be patient and let the mold <u>dry for two days</u>. If the mold is not completely dry the fused fired glass will stick to the kiln wash and chunks of the fiberboard may be pulled out on removal as well. To prevent this sticking, the mold must be totally dry before firing. We feel that air-drying is better but some crafters like to speed up the process by curing the primer coated mold in a warm kiln (be sure to vent the kiln) soaking it at 300°F (150°C) for approximately 3 hours. Turn off the kiln and let it cool to room temperature.

8. Use glass colors that will compliment your frog design and you don't have to stick to green! Cut the glass into strips approximately 1/4" (6.4) wide. Clean these strips using dishwashing soap and warm water. Be sure to dry each piece thoroughly.

9. Now the strips need to be broken in smaller square pieces. You can create these smaller pieces using a mosaic cutter or by scoring and breaking (remember that you will need to clean the cutter oil off the frit if you use this alternate method). Please see step 7 & 8 on page 57 for more details on this frit making process.

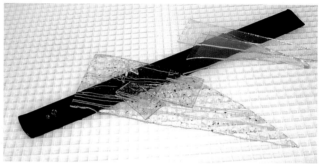

10. Next place the small glass pieces into the mold. Remember to place the various colors in a pattern that will be 'frog-like'. Use enough glass frit pieces to fill the mold approximately three glass layers thick.

11. The photo at right shows the finished glass-loaded mold. Notice the two pre-fired dichroic nuggets that we carefully placed for the frog's eyes (see project 6, page 40 for instructions on making these handy little nuggets).

12. Place the completed assembly into your kiln and fire the frog using the firing chart on page 58 for Frit Casting - Full Fuse - 2-3 Layers.

13. When the kiln has cooled to room temperature remove the mold & frog and carefully extract the cast frog from the mold. Dunk the frog into your water bucket to remove the primer particles then hold the mold upside down over the bucket and tap the side of the mold to dislodge the loose particles into the water.

14. You may find a few spikes around the edge of your fired piece (as we did in the frit cast dolphin steps 14 & 15 pages 58 & 59). Remove these points using an abrasive stone or glass grinder then fire polish your piece to give it that professional touch.

15. An optional step to make your frog into a three-dimensional standing sculpture. Carve a piece of fiberboard into a low profile egg-shape and drape the frog over the mold while fire polishing. The legs will bend down and flatten out on the kiln shelf. Now your frog can stand on his/her own 4 feet. Use the firing polishing chart provided below left to drape and polish the frog at the same time.

Place a piece of Thinfire™ release under the frog mold prior to firing the kiln.

MEDIUM COMPONENTS - FIRE POLISH - 1/4" (6MM) THICK

Phase	Temp/Min	Arrive Temp	SoakTime	Action
Temp Up	5°F / 3°C	1000°F / 538°C	1 min	Remove Vent
Temp Up	Full-speed	*1350°F / 732°C	10+/- min	Observe
Flash Cool	High-speed	1100°F / 593°C	0 min	Open & Close Lid
Temp Hold	5°F / 3°C	955°F / 513°C	45 min	Hold your fire
Temp Down	3°F / 2°C	750°F / 400°C	1 min	Do Not Peek
Cool Down	Undisturbed	100°F / 38°C	N/A	Do Not Peek

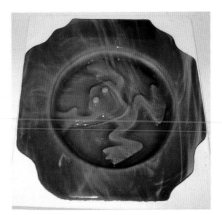

This plate was made by cutting the design from a piece of fiber paper and draping a single layer of glass over it.

* 'Arrive' Temperature will vary; it is essential to 'Observe' your project carefully as it approaches.

The eyes, eyebrows and smiley upturned mouth are provided for illustration and amusement only. Please do not try to carve these features into the mold form.

HotTip

At the beginning of my fusing career I encountered many broken pieces when I opened the kiln. Often the pieces were broken into two or three chunks with nice rounded edges. Today I know that this is an indication that the incident happened during the ramp up phase. I would try to slump fire a two or three layer thick pre-fused piece at the same ramp-up speed that I used for the original fuse firing. Occasionally I'd get away with it, but not often. Then I took a class from Newy Fagan and she taught me a rule of thumb that I use all the time, 'ramp up at half the speed of the previous firing'. For example if you used 15°F (9°C) per minute ramp speed for the fuse firing, then ramp up 8°F (5°C), approximately half speed, for the slump firing.

Introduction to Glass Fusing

Project 12 - Soup Bowls

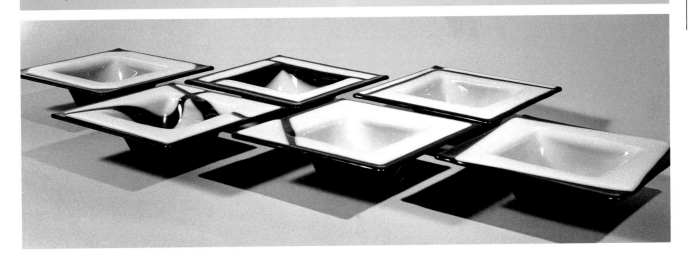

A few years ago we took a little vacation time to visit Chalet Suzanne, an unusual resort in west-central Florida. Their restaurant is famous for the celebrities they have served (they have photos everywhere). You quickly understand why, when you experience their fabulous 5-course dinner. One of the courses is a delicious soup that they serve in stunning hand-made ceramic bowls, that intensifies the experience of eating this soup.

We found out later that this soup was prepared right out of a can! Turns out the owners have a soup factory on the resort property, which we toured the following day and purchased some of their 'soups in a can' to take home with us. We decided that we needed some special soup bowls to create our own unique presentation for these wonderful soups.

What You'll Learn

- Make slump mold from fiberboard (we're using Kaiser-Lee™ board)
- Setting up a drop-out mold
- Procedure for slumping 2" deep

Tools & Equipment

- Glass cutting tools
- Glass cleaning supplies
- Kiln, kiln controller and shelf
- Putty knife - 3" (7.6 cm) stainless steel blade
- A paper nail file or sanding block
- Aluminum Baker's Tray (optional)

Materials

- Glass (either COE but all glass must be the same) 1 piece of the following for each bowl:
    - 6 3/4" (17 cm) square Black opal for the base
    - 6" (15.2 cm) square, White opal for the décor
- Fiberboard (Kaiser-Lee™ Board) 1" x 8" x 9" (2.5 x 20 x 23 cm)
- Kiln & Shelf, medium/large size - 8" x 8" (20 x 20 cm) or larger

Chalet Suzanne is famous for the their fabulous 5-course dinners that include a delicious soup that they serve right out of a can! We decided that we needed some special soup bowls to create our own unique presentation.

Step-By-Step Instructions

1. Fiberboard is delicate and will break easily so we must handle it with care. Place the board on a flat and even surface while working with it. We like to use an aluminum tray (a baker's sheet is shown in the photo) but a flat bench top covered with newspaper will work just as well. Use your mask & goggles for these steps.

2. We'll start with a standard stock-size piece of Kaiser-Lee™ Board that is 1" x 8" x 9" (2.5 x 20 x 23 cm). Draw a 7" x 7" (17.8 x 17.8 cm) square on one corner of the board. You can draw directly on the board with any pencil or felt marker.

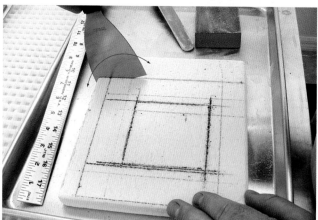

3. Next we'll use a putty knife to cut the 2" (5.1 cm) strip off the side. Put the knife on the cut line and press down on the knife while rocking it gently from side to side (see arrow in photo) until it sinks about 3/8" (1 cm) into the board. Remove the knife and move it along the line, repeat and continue all the way across. Turn the board upside down and tap on the side to remove the cutting-dust. Continue the same cutting process, moving slowly along the cut line 2 or 3 times until the knife has cut all the way through. Now do the same process to cut the 1" (2.5 cm) strip off of the other side. You'll use these 2 cutoff pieces as 'stilt bars' to raise the mold in the kiln.

4. Now draw a 4" x 4" (10.2 x 10.2 cm) square in the middle of the 7" x 7" (17.8 x 17.8 cm) board leaving a 1 1/2" (3.8 cm) perimeter rim border all around. This wide rim is important to prevent the glass from slipping down during firing. We want a solid square frame with a cutout in the center.

5. Now we'll cut the inside square using the putty knife as we did in step 3. However cutting an inside hole like this is a more delicate process than cutting off a strip and you must go very slowly. Press down gently on the knife and rock it from side to side (see arrow in photo) until it sinks about 3/8" (1 cm) into the board. Remove the knife and continue moving around the cut line several times until the knife has cut all the way through. Save the 4" (10.2 cm) square knock-out piece for future projects.

6. The final step is to use a finger nail file (a disposable paper file works just fine) to round the mold edges. All you need to do is blunt the sharp edges slightly, so 1 or 2 passes of the file will be sufficient. If an edge is rounded too much the glass could be drawn down unevenly during the slump firing.

Introduction to Glass Fusing

ProTip: When glass is slumped into a mold it actually stretches. The deeper the slump goes into the mold the thinner the glass becomes at the stretch area. Think of when you stretch bread dough or chewing gum. The stretch point gets thinner and eventually will break if pulled too much. The same action happens during glass slumping. There are two factors we can draw on to minimize thinning; one is the thickness of glass and the other is firing temperature and time

Thickness Factor:

The standard thickness of most art glass is 1/8" (3 mm). Some fusers use the rule-of-thumb of 1 layer per 2" (5 cm) of slump depth. However for tableware we need extra strength and for these items we like to use one layer per 1" (2.5) slump depth.

Temperature Factor:

The firing temperature for deep slumping (anything greater than 1" / 2.5cm) is much lower than the temperature for full or tack fusing (compare the slump schedule on pg 69, with the fuse schedule on pg 68).

(compare the slump schedule on pg 69, with the fuse schedule on pg 68).

> **HotTip**
>
> **Y**ou may ask; "Is it safe to use fused glass for dinnerware?" The official answer from the glass manufacturer's is "All tested compatible glasses have been tested by the FDA for food bearing surfaces and were determined to be suitable". However, if you add other processes or compounds to the items, for example paint, stains, decals, glazes, etc. it is important to check that these items are also approved for food bearing surfaces. In addition it is of the utmost importance that dinnerware items be properly annealed, especially if you're going to ladle in some hot soup - the thermal shock could cause a break in poorly annealed items.

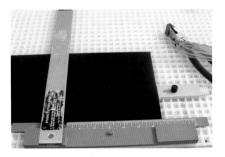

7. These bowls are going to be slumped 2" (5 cm) down through the mold we just made and that means we need 2 layers of glass for a thickness of at approximately 3/16" (4.8 mm). We'll need to do one firing to full-fuse the glass flat and a second firing to slump form the bowl.

8. All we did was cut one black glass 6 3/4" (17 cm) square and one white glass 6" (15 cm) square for each bowl. Then we divided the white glass into no more than 4 shapes. Often the simplest design is the most effective.

9. Clean the glass using dishwashing soap and warm water. Be sure to dry each piece thoroughly.

> **HotTip**
>
> **Y**ou might feel it would be nice to make an identical matched set of bowls. Experience tells us you can make a set that is close but chances are they will not look precisely alike. Instead we like to work with variations on a design to give the set of bowls individual character. So, we plan to make our designs different right from the beginning and people will appreciate our creativity as something special.

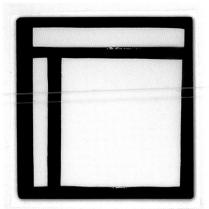
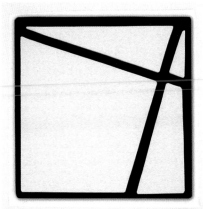

HotTip

Grinding the edge often causes devitrification and discoloration and this is especially noticeable on darker colors and iridized glass. Try to score and break the glass as close to your final shape as possible to minimize grinding or better yet avoid it altogether. This also occurs, if you use a diamond blade saw to cut your glass. One glass manufacturer explains it this way; "The roughened edges in the ground area creates thousands of tiny points from which crystal growth can easily propagate. This is referred to as 'edge-devit' (devitrification)". If you must grind, they suggest using a light coat of clear overglaze (i.e. Fusemaster Super Spray - also approved for food bearing surfaces) on the ground areas.

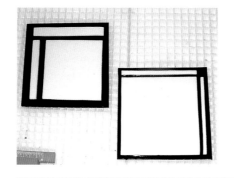

10. Assemble the glass parts according to your design and place it on a piece of Thinfire™ paper directly under each item you're firing or on a kiln shelf that has been primed using kiln wash. Place the shelf in the kiln, close the lid and do a full fuse firing. Follow the schedule provided here.

MEDIUM COMPONENTS - FULL FUSE - 2 LAYERS

Phase	Temp/Min	Arrive Temp	SoakTime	Action
Temp Up	12°F / 7°C	1000°F / 538°C	1 min	Remove Vent
Temp Up	Full-speed	*1480°F / 805°C	10+/- min	Observe
Flash Cool	High-speed	1100°F / 593°C	0 min	Open & Close Lid
Temp Hold	5°F / 3°C	955°F / 513°C	30 min	Hold your fire
Temp Down	3°F / 2°C	750°F / 400°C	1 min	Do Not Peek
Cool Down	Undisturbed	100°F / 38°C	N/A	Do Not Peek

* 'Arrive' Temperature will vary; it is essential to 'Observe' your project carefully as it approaches.

11. After the kiln has cooled to room temperature, remove the pre-fused flat plates and wash them in your dunk bucket to remove any remains of the Thinfire™ paper or shelf primer.

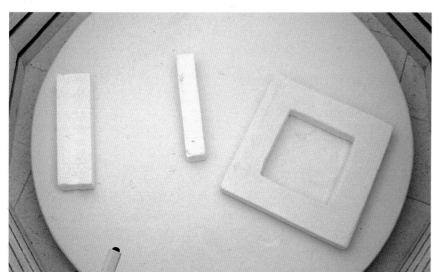

12. Next we will set up the mold for the slump firing. Place the 1" x 7" (2.5 x 17.8 cm) and the 2" x 8" (5.1 x 20.3 cm) fiberboard pieces on the kiln shelf. Make sure they are both turned so the topside of the fiberboard is up, to ensure the two 'stilt-bars' are the same height.

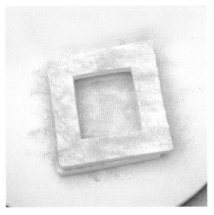

13. Place the mold on the bars so the stilts are in the center of the perimeter edge - it is important that they are 'set back' from the center opening.

14. Now use a sifter/strainer or your primer filled nylon stocking to sprinkle dry shelf primer on the mold and the kiln shelf through the center opening.

15. Place one of the pre-fused flat plates on the mold, make sure it is centered, then close the kiln lid and follow the schedule for slump firing presented below.

16. Slumping temperatures vary from kiln to kiln. Over time and with experience you will get to know the optimum slumping temperature for your kiln. In my favorite kiln it is between 1290°F and 1350°F (700°C - 732°C). If I go higher than 1350°F (732°C) the side 'stretch' areas of my slumped glass items become to thin. You must learn to be patient and let the glass slump down slowly. Once you have reached the slumping temperature open the kiln lid and take a peek (remember to wear your hi-temp kiln gloves and safety glasses when you do this). It's critical for you to stay close to the kiln during this step and keep checking every 8 to 10 minutes or so, until a flat bottom has formed on the bowl. When you are satisfied with the result, stop further slumping by venting the kiln until the temperature is down to 1100°F (593°C) then close the lid and allow it to cool and anneal according to the firing chart at left.

17. These bowls require careful annealing and cool down due to the thickness of glass in each bowl. Be sure to control the Temp Hold - anneal soak and the slow Temp Down to 750°F (400°C).

MEDIUM COMPONENTS - 2" DEEP SLUMP - 2 LAYERS				
Phase	*Temp/Min*	*Arrive Temp*	*SoakTime*	*Action*
Temp Up	6°F / 4°C	1000°F / 538°C	1 min	Remove Vent
Temp Up	Full-speed	*1300°F / 705°C	20+ min	Observe
Flash Cool	High-speed	1100°F / 593°C	0 min	Open & Close Lid
Temp Hold	5°F / 3°C	955°F / 513°C	30 min	Hold your fire
Temp Down	3°F / 2°C	750°F / 400°C	1 min	Do Not Peek
Cool Down	Undisturbed	100°F / 38°C	N/A	Do Not Peek

* 'Arrive' Temperature will vary; it is essential to 'Observe' your project carefully as it approaches.

Photo left: This is a simple flat fused glass design installed in a commercially available wooden jewelry box. An easy project and a beautiful presentation!

Photo right: This sculptural creation is in fact a happy accident. It was originally going to be a bowl but it turned out to be a interesting wall sculpture.

Introduction to Glass Fusing

Project 13 – Lidded Bowl

A good friend of ours collects lidded containers. We gave her a glass & wood jewelry box for her birthday one year that we made by adding a fused glass panel to a 'kit box' (a finished box with an opening in the lid) that is available from most art glass suppliers (see photo of this box on page 69, bottom left). For her next birthday we needed something different. So I came up with an idea for a lidded container made entirely from glass. Our friend loved it and we think you will too.

What You'll Learn

- Modifying the soup bowl mold with fiber paper to create a lid rim
- Making a lid, sized to fit
- Making a lifter knob for the lid
- Fusing and slumping in the same firing

Tools & Equipment

- Glass cutting tools
- X-acto™ knife (for fiber)
- Glass cleaning supplies
- Kiln, kiln controller and shelf

Materials

- Glass (any glass - see 'Note about glass' at right):
  - 7" x 7" (18 x 18 cm) for bowl
  - 4 1/2" x 4 1/2" (11.4 x 11.4 cm) for lid
  - Small pieces for lifter knob
- Fiberboard drop out mold, same mold we used for the soup bowl, project 12 - pg 66
- Fiber paper - 1/8" x 7" x 7" (4 mm x 18 x 18 cm)
- Thinfire™ paper or dry shelf primer
- E-6000™ adhesive

Note about the glass for this project:

We used a blue/green streaky glass for both the bowl and lid but you could use any color you wish or a different color for each piece. In fact, since we are simply slumping and fire polishing this project and not actually fusing any glass together, you could even use non-tested compatible glass (that is art glass that was not 'tested compatible' to be COE 90 or COE 96). The only problem you may encounter would be 'devitrification' - that is when the surface develops a haze and loses it's shine. Some glasses have a greater tendency to devitrify than others. It is advisable to do a full fuse test firing by stacking a couple of smaller pieces together. This will tell you how well the glass fuses and if it holds its shine or not. One other caution, if you do decide to use non-tested compatible glass, do not attempt to fuse it to any other glass (fuse it only to itself) or to decorate it with other glass components (i.e. dichroic). And remember to mark it as 'non-tested compatible' and store it in a place away from your tested compatible selections.

Step-By-Step Instructions

1. We will use the 7" x 7" (17.8 x 17.8 cm) mold with the 4" x 4" (10.2 x 10.2 cm) square drop out center hole (from the soup bowl project). If you didn't make the mold yet please see steps 1 to 6 on page 66.

2. We need to create a rim on this bowl for the lid to rest on, so we'll modify the mold with a piece of 1/4" (6 mm) thick fiber paper. Cut a 7" x 7" (17.8 x 17.8 cm) square piece then cut a 5" x 5" (12.7 x 12.7 cm) square hole in the center. This will give you a square fiber paper frame with a 1" (2.5 cm) outside border.

3. Place this fiber paper frame on top of the mold and place that on a kiln shelf in the kiln. If your kiln is large enough, place the mold to one side to allow room on the shelf to fire the lid at the same time. Do not place this mold on the stilt blocks as we did for the soup bowls. This bowl will only be 1" (2.5 cm) deep.

4. Cover the whole mold assembly with a 7" x 7" (17.8 x 17.8 cm) piece of Thinfire™ paper to act as a release or dust the mold and the center area of the shelf with kiln wash (as we did in the soup bowl project).

5. Now cut one 6 1/2" x 6 1/2" (16.5 x 16.5 cm) square glass for the bowl. Clean it using dishwashing soap and warm water and place it on the center of the mold inside the kiln.

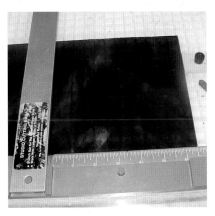

6. Cut another piece of the same glass 4 3/4" x 4 3/4" (12.1 x 12.1 cm) square that will become the lid. Clean this glass and dry it thoroughly. All we need to do with the lid is fire-polish the edges. If your kiln can accommodate it, you could do this in the same firing as the bowl itself. Remember to use a prepared shelf or place a piece of Thinfire™ paper on the shelf under the lid glass.

7. Fire the kiln following the firing schedule provided here.

8. After the kiln has cooled to room temperature remove the glass and clean it in your dunk bucket. The final step is to create and attach the lifter knob. We have used an assortment of items for the lifter knobs. Most often we simply stack 2 or 3 nuggets on the lid using E-6000™ glue.

ProTip: You could use an actual drawer pull or an interesting glass jewel, a bead or even a marble. You could attach a found object, such as an out of the ordinary stone or a seashell. This is one of those times when you should 'think outside of the box'.

9. Voilà! - that's it; and you don't have to tell anybody how easy it is.

MEDIUM COMPONENTS - 1" DEEP SLUMP - 1 LAYER				
Phase	*Temp/Min*	*Arrive Temp*	*SoakTime*	*Action*
Temp Up	15°F / 9°C	1000°F / 538°C	1 min	Remove Vent
Temp Up	Full-speed	*1430°F / 777°C	10+/- min	Observe
Flash Cool	High-speed	1100°F / 593°C	0 min	Open & Close Lid
Temp Hold	5°F / 3°C	955°F / 513°C	15 min	Hold your fire
Cool Down	Undisturbed	100°F / 38°C	N/A	Do Not Peek

* 'Arrive' Temperature will vary; it is essential to 'Observe' your project carefully as it approaches.

Project 14 - Candle Holder

Most art glass companies produce a selection of iridescent glass, but much of it is not available as tested compatible and therefore it cannot be combined with the standard fusible glass varieties. In addition the iridescent coating on non-tested compatabile glass often burns off (disappears) during firing if it is fired with the coated side up. However, if you fire with the iridescent side down - that is toward the kiln shelf - it usually stays. An additional benefit to firing with the coated side down is that the iridescent coating acts as a separator if you fire on Thinfire™ paper, fiber paper or fiberboard.

What You'll Learn

- Firing iridescent glass - coated side down
- Making a mold from recycled fiber paper

Tools & Equipment

- Glass cutting tools
- Tweezers or a small screwdriver
- Glass cleaning supplies
- Kiln, kiln controller and shelf

Materials

- Glass (any glass - see 'Note about glass' pg 70):
  - 7" x 7" (18 x 18 cm) iridized cathedral
- Fiberboard drop out mold, same mold we used for the soup bowl, project 12 - pg 66
- Fiber paper - small amount of previously fired paper

Step-By-Step Instructions

1. We are going to use the aluminum cup from an empty tea-light candleholder to create a core mold. This is a great way to recycle some 'already-fired' fiber paper. Used fiber paper is much softer and easier to pack into the cup. Press as much paper into the holder as you can, bearing down firmly to make sure it is tightly compressed. Then use tweezers, a sharp stick or a small screwdriver to poke through the bottom of the cup and force the fiber paper mold out.

HotTip

The iridized side is easy to identify on most colored glass but when using clear iridized it can be more difficult. If you're having trouble telling for sure then use the 'fingernail test'. Place the glass on a dark background and touch the surface with the tip of your finger. If the mirror image of your finger is directly under your finger then you have the iridescent side up. However, if the mirror image is 1/8" (3 mm) lower than your fingertip, you have the iridescent side down (if you don't know what this is all about, try touching your finger to both sides of the clear iridized glass and you will instantly see how this works).

2. Once again we will use the 7" x 7" (17.8 x 17.8 cm) mold with the 4" x 4" (10.2 x 10.2 cm) square drop out center hole (see steps 1 to 6 on page 66). Place the fiberboard mold on your kiln shelf and then place the fiber paper core mold piece you just created in the center hole of the mold.

3. Now cut a 6 3/4" X 6 3/4" (17 x 17 cm) piece of iridescent clear glass (or any color of iridized you choose). Clean and dry the glass, then place it on the mold, iridescent side down. For this project we are going to take advantage of the fact that firing with the iridescent coated side down will not stick to fiber paper or fiberboard. Since we are also going to use a fiberboard kiln shelf we do not have to use kiln wash or Thinfire™ release paper for this project at all.

4. Fire the candleholder according to the firing schedule presented here.

5. Finish the piece by gluing four clear plastic protective pads to the bottom corners of the candleholder (these items are available from your glass supplier or from office supply stores).

Phase	Temp/Min	Arrive Temp	SoakTime	Action
Temp Up	15°F / 9°C	1000°F / 538°C	1 min	Remove Vent
Temp Up	Full-speed	*1410°F / 766°C	10+/- min	Observe
Flash Cool	High-speed	1100°F / 593°C	0 min	Open & Close Lid
Temp Hold	5°F / 3°C	955°F / 513°C	15 min	Hold your fire
Cool Down	Undisturbed	100°F / 38°C	N/A	Do Not Peek

MEDIUM COMPONENTS - STANDARD SLUMP - 1 LAYER

* 'Arrive' Temperature will vary; it is essential to 'Observe' your project carefully as it approaches.

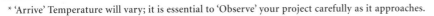

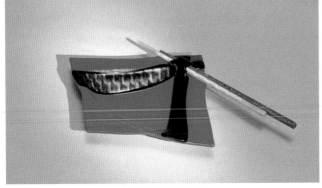

This single serving sushi plate was flat fused using a piece of fiber paper to create the space for the chopstick holder. Then it was slumped fired over a 1/4 circle fiberboard mold. Do not remove the fiber paper spacer until after the slump firing.

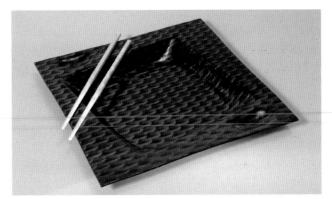

This dish was created from a single layer of black glass with a patterned iridized coating. It was simply slumped into 1" (2.5 cm) deep drop out fiberboard mold. We carved 2 small round bottom depressions in the mold to create the sauce holders.

Project 15 - Business Card Holder

We will use draping to shape the glass for this project. Previously we have used slumping where the glass is heated 1300°F to 1350°F (705°C to 730°C) until it stretches into the mold. The critical temperature for draping is lowered to between1200°F and1250°F (650°C - 675°C) relying on the weight of the overhanging glass to help bend it down.

This lower temperature means the edges of the glass will not fire polish or round off. If you're draping a pre-fused piece it will already have fire polished and rounded edges (that's exactly what we did for the blue and the pink swirl holders in the photo at right). However, if you are draping a flat piece that was not pre-fused and you want a rounded smooth edge (and who doesn't?) you must 'cold-polish' the edge prior to firing.

What You'll Learn

• Making a drape mold with fiberboard

• Preparing the mold for firing

• Polishing glass with diamond hand pads

• Firing schedule for draping

Tools & Equipment

• Glass cutting tools

• Diamond Coated Polishing Pads

• Sanding Block or paper nail file

• Glass cleaning supplies

• Kiln, kiln controller and shelf

Materials

• Glass (any glass - see 'Note about glass' pg 70):

  - 3 1/2" x 5" (9 x 13 cm) iridized cathedral or prefused piece with design

• Fiberboard 1" x 4" x 4" draping mold - this is the Fiberboard center cutout section from the soup bowl project on page 65

• Thinfire™ paper - sized to fit the glass

Step-By-Step Instructions

1. The drape mold we will use is the center cutout section from the soup bowl project (on page 65). Smooth all side edges of the mold using the sanding block or paper nail file. Then cover it with Thinfire™ paper to ensure easy removal after firing. It is better to use Thinfire™ paper as your mold release rather than kiln washing the mold because if the glass pinches and grips onto mold during drape firing the Thinfire™ paper disintegrates and acts as a buffer making removal easier.

2. Cut a piece of glass (we're using iridescent clear) that is approximately 3 1/2" x 5" (9 x 13 cm). That is just the right size for a business card holder. If you want to make a napkin or letter holder simply adjust the size of the glass and your mold.

These sponge-like buffing blocks are made by 3M and are color coded from coarse (black) to fine (blue) diamond grit.

Introduction to Glass Fusing

3. Since the glass in our project has not been pre-fired we will have to cold-polish the edges. You could use your glass grinder to remove and round off the corner edges but a more refined professional looking edge is possible by using diamond coated polishing pads. This product, manufactured by 3M, is a flexible sponge-like block with a layer of fine diamond grit on one side and available in a variety of grit sizes. Start with the coarse pad and submerge both the glass and pad in a pan of clean water. Use light pressure until you have determined a satisfactory cut rate. Continue to polish, stepping down to medium then finer grades until you have reached a top-quality finish.

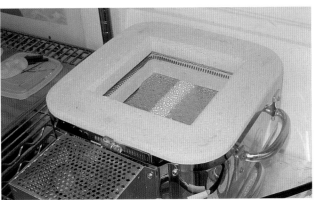

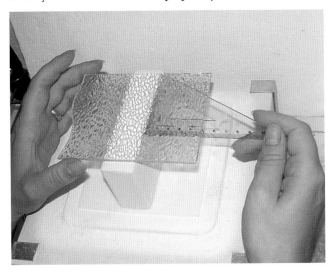

4. For this project we used our little Hot Box Kiln. Place the mold, covered with the piece of Thinfire™ paper, in the center of your kiln shelf. Thoroughly clean and dry the glass and lay it on top of the mold. Make sure it is positioned on the mold so you will get the desired business card holder shape.

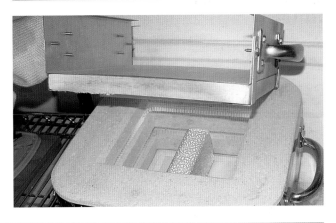

ProTip: Glass draping is best done one project at a time (this also applies to deep slumping). If you try to drape (or slump) several pieces in a larger kiln often one of the project pieces will achieve the desired shape while the others may still need some time. The problem is if you wait until everything is finished, the first piece(s) may very well be over-fired.

5. Close the kiln and fire it according to the schedule here for a standard drape firing.

MEDIUM COMPONENTS - STANDARD DRAPE - 1 LAYER				
Phase	*Temp/Min*	*Arrive Temp*	*SoakTime*	*Action*
Temp Up	15°F / 9°C	1000°F / 538°C	1 min	Remove Vent
Temp Up	Full-speed	*1230°F / 666°C	10+/- min	Observe
Flash Cool	High-speed	1100°F / 593°C	0 min	Open & Close Lid
Temp Hold	5°F / 3°C	955°F / 513°C	15 min	Hold your fire
Cool Down	Undisturbed	100°F / 38°C	N/A	Do Not Peek

* 'Arrive' Temperature will vary; it is essential to 'Observe' your project carefully as it approaches.

Introduction to Glass Fusing

Chapter 9 – Troubleshooting Questions And Answers

Blotchy, hazy surface coating

Q: My fused glass piece has a blotchy, hazy coating that looks like something was etched on the surface and I can't clean off. What is it and how can I solve this problem?

A: This hazy coating is called 'devitrification', and it is just as you describe it. Almost any glass will devitrify if it is held between 1000°F to 1300°F (593°C to 705°C) for too long. Some glass types are more prone to this problem than others, especially non-tested compatible glass. See; 'Note about the glass for this project' on page 70. In addition fumes in the firing chamber can cause hazing when binders, fiber paper, shelf paper or glue residue burns off. If you forget to vent your kiln, the fumes have no way to escape and will come back down onto your glass. Finally glass that was not cleaned properly or cleaned with the wrong solution will exhibit signs of hazing, even fingerprints can leave spots that appear to be 'etched into the surface'.

Black spots inside of the glass

Q: I made a plate, using several colors of cathedral glass layered together in a pattern. After firing I found black spots that are on the inside of the glass and a few black bubbles as well. What caused this and can I fix it?

A: Could it be that you used glue to fix your décor pieces to the base glass? We try to use as little glue as possible and fire the glass as soon as possible. I use glue and so do my students and we usually have good success. But I've found that the longer I leave the assembled glass before I fire it the more likely I am to get black spots between the layers.

Ugly gray edges

Q: I fused a plate with a red opal background and used iridized black glass to create a strip design across the surface. The design looks fabulous in the finished fired piece but these ugly, hazy, gray edges have appeared along the black strips. Why did this happen?

A: Sounds to me like you used your grinder or a diamond saw to shape those black glass strips before firing. You have encountered 'devitrification' please see HotTip on page 68 and ProTip on page 30 for an explanation of this 'ugly edge' problem and how to avoid it in the future.

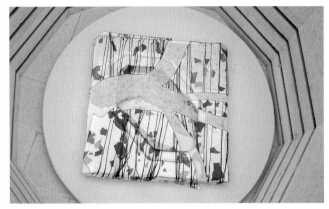

Glass was broken into 5 pieces

Q: I was trying to make a 1" deep plate using a single layer of glass that has fractures and streamers already in it. I placed the glass on the mold and closed the kiln lid and left it closed (I promise I didn't look) until the kiln was at 1300 °F and when I opened the lid to check the glass it was already broken into 5 pieces (see photo above). What happened?

A: The rounded edge on the glass indicates the crack happened during the Temp Up phase. You should consider using a 2 layers thick slumping chart (the fractures and streamers are a 'sort of' layer) to reduce the Temp/Min ramp speed in phase one. See ProTip about ramp up speed on page 59.

Bottom is not very flat

Q: I made a set of the soup bowls with a 2" deep slump (see project 12 on page 65 in this book). The bottom on some of the bowls is not very flat and they tip over easily while others are just fine. I tried to do them all exactly the same way. Can you think of anything that I may have done incorrectly? I should tell you that I did slump fire them 2 at a time in my 22" octagon kiln.

A: Kilns are notorious for having hot and cold spots in them. The larger the kiln, the more likely this is to occur. The bowl that is not flat enough didn't fully slump, because it was in a colder spot than the bowl that did fully slump. The fix is to fire only one bowl at a time (see ProTip on page 75). Experienced fusers can successfully slump more than one item at a time but it requires carefully placing and checking during the firing cycle. Your bowls that are "not very flat and tip over easily" can be fixed by refiring to slump them fully this time – but make sure they are very clean before you refire!

Bubbles ruined my plate

Q: I made a plate using a bottom layer of black opal then I added a layer of décor pieces and finished it off with a clear layer. I took the plate to full fuse temperature of 1470°F and let it soak for 10 minutes so the surface was completely flat. When I removed it the next day I found several bubbles under the clear glass. I could live with some of the smaller bubbles but the bigger ones ruined my plate. What happened?

A: Bubbles are trapped air between the glass layers. Basically the edges of the glass layers seal before the air can escape. It is almost impossible to eliminate bubbles altogether but there are some things you can do to minimize them.

- Slow the ramp speed down between 1050°F to 1250°F (565°C to 675°C) to give the bubbles time to escape before the edges seal. Adding a 1/2 hour soak around 1200°F (650°C) may also help. This extra slow soak time is called a 'bubble squeeze'.
- Don't use a full-size piece of clear glass as the top layer, this will almost certainly trap air bubbles. Instead cut the clear top layer into smaller pieces to allow venting, the clear layer will combine to look like it was one piece after full fuse firing.
- Some fusers place a small 'lift glass' piece at the edge between larger glass layers. This holds the edge up a little longer allowing the center to slump first and giving the air bubbles an escape avenue.
- It also depends on the way you place your décor pieces. Sometimes air has no way of getting out. We very seldom cover our décor with a clear glass. In your case we would have topped the black glass with the clear and placed the décor on top.

Huge blister-bubble

Q: I made a beautiful cat design and thought I did everything correctly. I cleaned all the pieces and dried them well, I didn't use any glue to hold the components. I used my clay kiln shelf with a new coating of kiln wash and I even put Thinfire™ paper on my kiln shelf. Then I ramped the kiln up according to a schedule that worked before and let it cool overnight. I was really disappointed the next day when I opened the kiln and found this huge blister-bubble that formed between my glass and the kiln shelf (I've enclosed a photo). Why did this happen to me – I've tried to live a good life?

A: Bubbles like this are too big to be trapped air, instead they are caused by a process called 'gassing off'. Something under the glass turned into a gas

while in the slumping temperature range. It could be an organic material (like dirt) but most likely it was caused by moisture. Thinfire™ paper can help to prevent this, so you must have really had a bunch of something under there to have this happen (actually your cat looks like he could have been a trumpet player). I'm sure you think you let the kiln shelf dry completely but I suspect there was still some moisture in there that caused this gassing to occur. My best recommendation is to use a fiber-board shelf (of course we use Kaiser-Lee™ board) since this porous material allows the gas and air to escape. Also you may have a bad batch of kiln wash or one that had a reaction to something in your kiln.

A way to make bubbles happen on purpose

Q: I fused some 2-layer pendants and found some bubbles trapped inside and between the layers of glass. I actually like how they look and would like to know if there is a way to make them happen on purpose?

A: Bubbles are usually created when air is trapped between glass layers during firing. Since art glass often has a rough side you could try placing the two rough sides against each other and chances are you will end up with some small bubbles. The bubbles you found could have come from using a glass that already had bubbles in it from the original manu-facturing process (these bubbles are called seeds). I have heard that some adventurous fusers place assorted organic materials between the glass layers on purpose to (hopefully) create bubbles due to 'gassing off' (see previous question). I have tried using baking soda but the results were erratic and I stopped trying. If you have time, why not do some research and testing to find a suitable organic material, you could make an exciting discovery – but please be careful what you put in the kiln.

Hoping for an interesting 'flowing' effect

Q: I have a beautiful clay-mold that I've used many times to slump serving sized plates. I knew enough to put lots of shelf primer on it and let it dry completely. I had an idea to slump a 2 layered, pre-fired piece of glass on it. I intentionally made the glass slightly larger than the mold so it would 'run over' the edge. I was hoping it would produce an interesting 'flowing' effect. Unfortunately when I took the fired piece out of the kiln I could not release it from the mold plus I discovered a crack in the glass. Can you tell me why?

A: Working with bisque-fired clay molds has its own set of rules. One of these rules is; only fire 'into' clay molds. This means slumping 'into' the mold was fine; it was the draping 'over' where things went wrong. This has to do with expansion, contraction and other rules of physics but it doesn't matter why it happened, just that you really shouldn't try it. Unfortunately you had to learn 'why' you shouldn't the hard way.

Kiln wash stuck on the bottom

Q: I made a disk using a yellow opal bottom layer with some décor pieces on top. I took the kiln up slowly to full fuse temperature of 1490°F (810°C). The next day I opened the kiln and it looked beautiful until I picked it up and found sharp spikes sticking out around the perimeter plus kiln wash stuck to several places on the back. I took the spikes off with my grinder (and now the edge has grinder marks) but I couldn't get the kiln wash off no matter what I tried. What went wrong and how do I make sure this doesn't happen in the future?

A: The spikes are usually the result of over firing either too hot or too long at full fuse temperature. Each kiln is different and you'll need to adjust your full fuse temperature accordingly. As for the stuck kiln wash, opalescent glass is prone to kiln wash sticking and the over firing added to the sticking problem. We like to use Thinfire™ shelf paper as our release because it almost never sticks plus we use a fiberboard shelf and that also helps reduce the problem. If you must use kiln wash we recommend Primo™ Primer, it really reduces the incidence of sticking and as a bonus it cleans off the shelf easily. Finally, you can try cleaning really stubborn kiln wash using CLR™ cleaner or Limeaway™ cleaner. They don't always work but it's worth a try. The ultimate 'stubborn kiln wash' cleaner is a sand-blaster. This will definitely clean the kiln wash off plus it will leave a frosted etched bottom.

Do you have a question?

Send it to me at kaiserlee@earthlink.net and I'll try to send you an answer. Who knows, your question might make it into a future fusing book!

Here is one final answer - The answer to the Tangram pictograms on page 24. Sure, it looks easy now but try it without the solutions!

Wardell
PUBLICATIONS INC

email: info@wardellpublications.com
website: www.wardellpublications.com